ALSO BY KELLEY (Kelly) R. PORTER

Perfectly Planned Workbook and Audiobook (Overcoming Incest, Rape & Sexual Abuse)

Overcoming Toxic Relationships (Creating Power from Past Pain)

Mental MakeOver (Creating a Positive Mindset) Book of Quotes

It's All About Life: Book of Poems

Detox or DIEt (Closing the Gap Between Dis-ease and Death)

PERFECTLY Planned
OVERCOMING INCEST, RAPE & SEXUAL ABUSE

"CELEBRATE LIFE AFTER ABUSE"
Kelley R. Porter

KELLEY R PORTER, CERTIFIED LIFE COACH

Reviews

"Interesting, truthful and heartfelt. Very inspirational novel; one that should be read in his quest to bounce back to the love that life has to offer."
Uncle Rail Radio Personality/Comedian

"PERFECTLY PLANNED simply moved me to tears. After reading this I could not help but make sure my secure relationship with my children and especially my daughters were undoubtedly unbreakable. Kelley has pinned an amazing piece that will give hope to the abused, awareness to the unknown and strength to the survivors."
Zurek (Rick Party) Radio Personality

Kelley Porter's first novel gives readers a real-life adventure that is almost too fascinating to be real. Passage after passage, Ms. Porter not only draws the reader deeper into the story; she causes the reader to feel the emotions -highs and lows, as well as the pain. This tone has a hard core, heartfelt truthfulness that can only be told by someone who has lived through and survived the many ordeals the author presents.
Glenn Reedus, Managing Editor, Crusader Newspaper Group

Kelley R. Porter is a modern day Harriet Tubman leading others from their captivity of molestation. This is what a champion looks like. A champion has opposition, and odds stacked against them, and challenges that make the average person weak at the knees. What a person has overcome determines if they are a champion or not. Kelley has overcome huge obstacles.
Toure Muhammad, Director - Bean Soup Times

PERFECTLY
Planned

OVERCOMING INCEST, RAPE & SEXUAL ABUSE

"CELEBRATE LIFE AFTER ABUSE"

Kelley R. Porter

COACH KELLEY
TRANSFORMING LIVES WORLDWIDE

Copyright ©MMIX by Kelley R. Porter

All rights reserved. Printed in the United States of America. No part of this book may be used or reproduced in any manner whatsoever without written permission except in the case of brief quotation embodied in critical articles and reviews. Nonfiction. Names have been changed for the protection of privacy.

Designed by Kelley Porter
Cover Design by Julie Holloway
Library of Congress Control Number: 2011913828
ISBN: 978-0-9851767-0-9

PORTER PUBLISHING
TRANSFORMING LIVES WORLDWIDE

Dedication

This book is dedicated to my parents as well as all victims and survivors who have suffered from sexual, verbal or physical abuse, incest and abandonment. Individuals who are also having a difficult time forgiving wrongdoers who have placed pain upon them.

The journey to freedom and forgiveness may be a long and exhausting one, but never give up on liberating yourself. Your role in life requires a forgiving heart because if not, a bitter heart will cause other's pain and block your blessings. This is the only way to live "whole" and not "broken"

From the mind of a child molester to the mouth of a child.

"Start the process of healing with forgiveness and end with deliverance."

Acknowledgments

I'd like to give a special acknowledgement to Pastor Ledbetter from Greater Mount Hebron Church for being there to listen on numerous occasions and praying for me.

A special acknowledgement to Josh Moore for calling me three years ago and suggesting I write this book, and share my life in an effort to help others.

Also, special thanks to Lonita Mondane, Angela Cowan, Paul (Supervisor), Aunt Pam, Annalisa Moo-Yin, and Daniel Davis for being so influential in my life when I so desperately needed someone. Thank you all for being God's angel.

I would also like to thank all my laboratory co-workers at Metro South Medical Center for being so supportive throughout my journey. Thank you all from the bottom of my heart.

Contents

1. Shattered Trust — 1
2. The Ring Leader — 3
3. Traumatized — 15
4. Abandoned — 24
5. Chester the Molester — 36
6. Reunion — 71
7. The Truth — 83
8. Devastated — 90
9. Desperately Seeking Love — 97
10. Ms. Sexable the College Student — 105
11. My First Love — 133
12. Reflecting Back and Moving Forward — 136
13. Forgiveness — 151
14. Survivor — 157
15. My Personal Thoughts — 162

I was fearful,
Now I am fearless,
I was silenced,
Now I am outspoken,
I was ordered to sit down,
Now I have the power to stand,
I broke the chains of adversity and
Now I have the keys to liberation.

~Patrick O. Turner

Shattered Trust-1

Dressed in a burgundy robe with colorful print until a few seconds later, Nippy exposed his dark, naked body to me. He smiled and all of his teeth showed, stacked on top of one another. His chest was covered in thick, black hair, and he had a pot belly. I gasped; I giggled and dropped my head to look at the black tiles covering the floor of my bedroom. When I looked up, he was gone. I was in shock. I was scared as a cat cornered by a dog. I laid Barbie and Ken on the floor and stood to my feet shaking. The force of my heartbeat was so physically powerful, I could hear it. My palms began to sweat. I nervously and hastily walked down that long hallway to the living room. Daddy sat at the table pushed against the wall with a two sided mirror, and tweezers picking the ingrown hairs from his face. Mama and some of my cousins were sitting on a black couch watching our black and white television.

"Daddy and Mama, Nippy just showed me his thing and naked body."
I was disgusted.
"Well, your fast ass shouldn't have been playing with him."
"I wasn't playing with him. I was playing with Barbie and Ken and he just came in the room, and opened his robe."
"Go sit your fast ass down somewhere."

Those were Daddy's last words as well as mine. Mama never spoke a word. I wondered why. I wondered why no one said anything. I stood there confused, lost, sad, angry, betrayed, and defeated. I was sure I didn't do anything wrong. But there I was, accused and sentenced to go sit my fast ass down.

Mama was remarkably small, but always a giant in my eyes. She was four feet eleven inches and a red-bone as black folk sometimes called fair-skinned black women. Mama had long, shiny "good" hair that caused envy among a lot of other black women in her younger days. Her cheekbones were so high and prominent that they framed her small, slanted eyes and spoke of her Native-American Heritage. She was fearless and would stand up to anybody to defend her family. She was very nice and gave you her last. Mama was extremely affectionate and loving, but she didn't play any games.

Mama volunteered at my Grammar school to ensure I was treated well and received the education she did not. She never missed a P.T.A meeting. She was a prominent member of our church and enjoyed helping others. (R.I.P I love you always; my greatest gift.)

Daddy was a stern father and believed in corporal punishment when it came to his family. He was taller than Mama and from what I heard, he physically abused her. Daddy was five feet, eleven inches, medium-build and wore bifocals. He was brown skinned with salt and pepper, short, curly hair. He also believed children were seen and not heard. He wasn't always happy and for the most part, his behavior was always aggressive, angry and defensive. However, he was my father and I loved him. (R.I.P I love you always; my hero)

The Ring Leader-2

Daddy and Mama never spoke another word of Nippy exposing his naked body to me. Later that day when Daddy and Mama were out, Daminea confronted Nippy and he denied the whole thing.

Nippy was known as Chester the Molester in the neighborhood and was very cunning, manipulative and deceitful. He gambled a lot and was very abusive. It was no secret he messed with young girls. He was twenty years old, about five feet eleven inches tall, dark-skinned, medium build, black short Afro, unattractive and paid Daddy one hundred, and fifty dollars to live in our apartment. Nippy was alleged to be my cousin, Damenia's boyfriend.

"Nippy, did you show Kelley your d*ck?" Daminea was angry.
"Hell naw. She's lying. She just wants some attention."
"Kelley you better not be playing with him. That's my boyfriend and I better not catch your ass talking to, or playing with him."
I felt my heart pound through my chest.
"Daminea, I wasn't playing with him. He just came in my room and showed me his thing."
"Get the hell out my face. I believe him and I better not catch your ass playing with him. Your ass just wants some attention."

Damenia was one of my older cousins. She was brown skinned with short hair and a lot taller than me. Before Nippy, we got along very well. She was always nice and I never thought she would make me do some of the things she did. Every day I had to look Nippy in his lying face. I despised him and wanted him out of our house.
"I'm going to get your younger cousins."
I didn't understand what Nippy meant, but I found out later.

Perfectly Planned   (Overcoming Incest, Rape & Sexual Abuse)

It was almost the end of summer. The sun was shining, the birds were singing, the grass was green and full with bright red tomatoes, light green cabbage, lettuce and collard greens. These were the best times. On the side-entrance of the building there was a courtyard almost half the size of a football field; two swing sets, monkey bars, sliding boards, strike out box, four corners and hopscotch painted yellow on the pavement. Everything a child wanted for a day of play. Some of the teenagers played softball and some played hopscotch. Children swung high on the swing-set.

"Kelley, it's your birthday, drink this."
It was nasty, but I drank it because Daminea said so. My stomach hurt and I vomited.
"Go lie down Kelley."
I looked down beside my bed, and there was a white bucket for me to spill my guts. I had my first taste of beer; Old English.

Weeks later, while I watched television, Daminea approached me and asked me to come into the last bedroom. She was thirteen years-old at the time. I got up and followed her into the bedroom. A bedroom that was about twelve by fifteen and some days felt like a five by five. The door closed behind me and what was to come, I never imagined. Daminea laid a blanket on the floor between the two twin-sized beds. She removed her clothes and proceeded to lie down.
"Come on and lick me."
Daminea opened her legs.
"I don't wanna."
I stared at Daminea's vagina.
"Do it. Do it!"
"I don't want to!"
Out of fear, I agreed, got on my knees and began licking.
"Lick the clitoris."
"Lick right there." Daminea spread her vagina to expose her clitoris.
"Can I stop?"
"No. Keep going."

I cried. I wanted to stop. Several minutes passed and there was a noise.
"Get up. Get up. Somebody's coming."
Daminea jumped up and dressed herself.
"You better not tell Daddy and Mama."
Daminea's voice threatened me. On numerous occasions, she gathered the younger girls and boys from the neighborhood and brought them into our bedroom and insisted on us performing sexual acts.
"Stand in line next to each other. Take off your clothes and lick each other's breast."
Daminea ordered me and some of my friends and I didn't resist. I did what Damenia said as I always did. I was always told I had to listen to my older cousins. During the summer of 1979, and at the innocent age of eight, I learned a lot about sex.

"Baby girl, wake up. It's your first day of school. Go wash your face, brush your teeth, get dressed and come eat breakfast."
"Okay.
"Did you piss in the bed last night?"
"Yeah."
I was nervous.
"Gimme the cord. I told your pissy ass to stop pissin in the bed!"
"Okay Daddy. Okay Daddy. I won't pee in the bed again!"
"Eat your got damn food before I whip your ass again!"
I finished my food and it was time for school. Daddy walked out the door and I walked behind him because I was mad.
"Bring your ass on."

There was total silence on the ride to school. I walked to the entrance of Carter G. Woodson Elementary school on forty fourth and Evans. I never spoke of anything that occurred in my home. I was a very intelligent child and always happy-go-lucky. Life at school was normal for me. I've always been anxious to help others, and loved attending school. It made me feel really good to help another classmate.

In the third grade, Mr. Thomas was my teacher. He was white, tall, brown hair, medium build and very nice. He dressed very well with his button down shirt, tie and slacks. I loved Mr. Thomas. He was so kind to us. He believed in us and used games and other activities to make us feel good about ourselves.

"Mama, I won a coloring book in school."
"Hey baby, how was school?"
"It was fun. I won a coloring book."
"Do your homework while I get dinner ready."
"Okay. What's for dinner Mama?"
"I made smothered fried chicken in gravy with rice, peas and Kool-Aid."
Mama grabbed the plates and Daddy walked in.
"Hey honey, come sit down and eat."
"Stop licking the damn plate. You're acting like a damn dog. Get your hungry ass away from the table!"
"Mama, can I go outside?"
"Yeah, and don't get in no trouble."

I grabbed a handful of rocks and walked across the courtyard and into the small forest across from our building. I climbed to the top of the tree where no one could see me. I waited for my friends to come outside and one by one, I threw rocks at them. They had no idea where it came from.

"Ouch. Ouch. Ouch. Somebody's throwing rocks. Man, y'all better stop playing."
I laughed so hard, tears filled my eyes and suddenly I became the target.
"That's Kelley in the tree."
I enjoyed my afternoon being a kid and safe in the tree, but it didn't last very long.

"Come in the house y'all. Come in the house with me."
"Okay, here we come."
I threw my rocks down and went in the house with Daminea.
"Come in the back."

We all followed Daminea to the back bedroom. I didn't notice my parents left again.
"Kiss Lamont Kelley."
I giggled. We kissed.
"Jes, take your clothes off."
"Kelley suck Jes's d*ck."
Jes pulled the skin back on his penis and there was a lot of white stuff on it. *That's nasty*. I thought.
"No, I don't wanna do that."
I frowned and turned my nose.
"Do it Kelley!"
"I'll go lookout so we don't get caught."
Daminea walked out the room and I continued to do what she what she told me. I wasn't sure what I was doing. So I licked Jes's penis. I was completely disgusted.
"Lamont, it's your turn. Kelley and Lamont take off your clothes and lie on the bed. Lamont get on top of Kelley and put your penis in."
 Lamont tried and tried as I laid there very scared.
"It hurts. I don't want to do it."
"Lamont stop. Go back outside."
Daminea made sure Mama and Daddy never knew about these things and would never find out. As time went by, I didn't think about telling. I started to enjoy the sexual acts, and explore more on my own.

My other cousins, Chrissy, Al and David were never at home either. Chrissy, the oldest cousin and was seven years older than me. She was light-skinned and a few inches taller. She was very intelligent and always dressed nice. I always thought she was mean to me. I didn't like how she made me and Nicki fight. I didn't think she liked me for whatever reason. Chrissy had no problem fighting when she needed to. She was one tough girl. David was a year younger than Chrissy, and six years older than me. He was about five feet-five inches, medium brown skinned, and very handsome with a beautiful smile. David was intelligent, helpful and nice.

He loved to sing and enjoyed doing back flips. He actually taught me to do a back flip. That one day in the winter of nineteen eighty one changed his entire life.

Allen was a tad bit taller than Chrissy and David. He was three years older than me, medium brown skinned, and always out with his friends. Allen wasn't around very much. Nicki was my favorite cousin. We hung together and I admired her. She was two years older than me, and very smart. Nicki was two inches taller and a little darker than me. She helped me with my homework and was very protective of me. As a matter of fact, in the beginning, they all protected me.

****

"Mama, I'm hungry."
"I made some oatmeal. Sit down and I'll make you a bowl."
"Can I have some milk?"
Mama removed a glass from the cabinet and poured my milk. The glass was half-empty and I wanted more. I accidentally knocked my glass of milk over and it spilled on Daddy's newspaper.
"What the f*ck is wrong with you? Ignoramus ass wet up my newspaper. Get your ass away from the table!"
I got up and went to my room. I put on my pink floral dress and pink shoes. I had six ponytails in my hair; three on each side. It was kind of frayed since those were the same pony tails Mama did last Sunday.
"Baby girl come back in here and finish your breakfast."
I finished my breakfast and off to church we went. After church, I grabbed my skates, went outside and enjoyed the pleasant breeze against my face. I squatted down and stuck one leg out and positioned my hands like a steering wheel. The motorcycle wasn't easy, but I mastered it. My skate wheel got stuck between a crack in the pavement and I flew face first to the ground. Instant reaction; my hands took control and landed on the pavement; no scratches and no bruises.
"Ah ha, Kelley fell y'all."
Roger was my friend and neighbor.

"So. I rolled my neck and continued to maneuver my way through and around the cracks, and disappeared like Casper the friendly ghost. I had fun until Damenia called me and some of my friends.
"Ya'll go ahead. I'll go look out for y'all."
Daminea taught us enough, so I guess she figured we knew what to do. One of my friends humped my body and another kissed my breast. My body felt different. I enjoyed it. I couldn't tell Mama and Daddy. I was scared they would blame me or Daminea would hit me. I started to think it was okay. I desired them and wanted to explore more. I didn't have the courage, so I didn't. I continued being a kid. I enjoyed the fun times and wanted the bad times to go away.

What would my Daddy and Mama think? Who would they blame? Would I be accused like before? Would they listen? Would my emotions be overlooked again? I thought.

I played outside for a while and asked Latrice to come inside with me. Latrice was one of my neighborhood friends, and she was one of the kids I experienced sexual acts with. She knew how to smoke cigarettes, and experienced sex prior to moving to our neighborhood. We immediately used Ken and Barbie to imitate what Daminea taught us. Latrice laid Ken on top of Barbie and I put Barbie's head between Ken's thighs. We giggled.
"Latrice let's freak."
"Okay."
Latrice laid down and I laid on top of her. I rolled my body onto hers, we kissed each other's breast, and rubbed on each other. My body felt like it did when Daminea made me perform these acts with other kids. Only this time, Daminea wasn't there and I did all that she taught me to do. The doorknob turned and we jumped up.
"What y'all doing in here?"
"We not doing nothing. We're just playing with Barbie and Ken."
"Go back outside and I'll call you when dinner is ready."

"Okay."
We went back outside and never talked about what we did. We continued on and played like nothing ever happened.
"Kelley!"
"Latrice, I gotta go in the house. I'll see you tomorrow after school."
"Mama, I'm home. Daddy said he was gonna pick me up from school and he didn't."
I was angry.
"That's okay. You made it home safely. Keep your coat on. You're going with me. Big Mama called and she said she got something for me."
Big Mama was like a second mother to Mama, and was kind and sweet. She was shorter, but a lot tougher than Mama. Big Mama's complexion was fair and she had a small round frame. Her hair was black and thinning.
"Hey Big Mama."
"Hey baby."
We hugged. I was happy to see her.
"Y'all hungry?"
Big Mama was so kind to us.
"Yeah."
"Dewitt keeps being an ass and throwing the food away."
"Why don't you leave that man?"
"I ain't got nowhere to go. Besides, I got all these kids to take care of."
"Here's a sandwich baby."
Big Mama gave me a salami sandwich, some Cheetos, and an apple juice.
"Kelley, I need you to help me carry these bags home."
We packed the bags.
"I'd like to see his ass try to throw this food out."
Mama was fierce sometimes.
"Well, he better not touch nothing I give you, or I'll come over there and see him."
Spoken like the champ Big Mama was.
"Here's a cart Janie. Y'all gotta walk a mile."
"Thanks, Big Mama."
"Thank you Big Mama."

****

"Where the hell you been?"
Daddy was mad Mama wasn't home when he got there.
"I went to see Big Mama."
"Oh, well cook me some dinner."
"Daddy, can I have a quarter?"
"Hell naw."
"Old grasshopper."

Daddy chewed tobacco and it smelled horrible. He kept a white bucket in his bedroom next to his bed so he could spit the brown fluid out that accumulated in his mouth. I wanted a quarter, so I could buy some candy, and I thought Daddy didn't hear me call him a grasshopper. I walked to my room and got into bed. Before I could process Daddy being so stingy, he slapped me directly on my cheek. That was my first and last time disrespecting Daddy.

I stayed in my bedroom and fell into a deep sleep. I felt Mama feeling around on my bed, and all of a sudden I was wrapped in pissy sheets and hauled out of bed.
"Didn't I tell you not to pee in the bed again?"
"Why you keep pissing in the bed?"
"Mama, I don't know why I pee in the bed. At night when I'm sleeping, I dream I'm on the toilet and pee. Sometimes I'm scared because it's so dark in here, and I'm afraid to come out of the room."
"Well, maybe you have a weak bladder. Go get ready for school." "Mama, I don't have a bath towel."
"Your Daddy used all of them to wipe his ass. Just find something and get cleaned up."
"Mama, I need some tissue?"
"Dee, I need some money for tissue."
"I ain't got no damn money."
There was a knock at the door.
"Who is it?"

Daddy answered the door and two tall, dark-skinned strangers with blue jeans, cowboy hats, and black jackets walked in.
"Cowboy, I want my damn money."
Cowboy was my Daddy's street name.
"I ain't got it."
"Cowboy if you don't pay me my damn money, I'll take your baby."
Mama grabbed me and put me behind her.
"You ain't taking my motherf*cking baby. I'll kill your ass. Now get the f*ck out my house."
The two men left and I was scared. Daddy and Mama argued again, but it didn't last long because Daddy had to take me to school. After school, I played in the courtyard until night fell. The sky was clear and filled with stars. The breeze was fresh and cool, and the crickets scratched their hind legs together, and spoke to each other. My curfew arrived. Mama and Daddy were not home.
"I gotta go in the house y'all, bye."
I approached the front entrance of my building and turned left. I came to an abrupt halt. I saw those same two men who visited Daddy earlier standing at our door. I stood there for about five seconds, and an adrenaline rush took over my body, and I turned and ran around the side of the building. Breathing hard and frightened as a tourist walking through the African Safari. I hid on the side of the building. I waited and waited until I saw them walk towards the houses west of my building. They became invisible and I ran as fast as I could, and made it safely into my house. I heard keys at the door and it was Mama and Daddy. I told Mama about those men and for some reason unknown to me; they never showed their faces around my building again.

****

"Come here Kelley and Latrice."
We ran over to see what Damenia wanted, and then walked a few blocks down from our building, and into another court way. Daminea took a Kool cigarette out and lit it.
"Take a pull, like this."

I took a pull and blew the smoke out.
"No, like this. You have to inhale the smoke."
I tried again, and this time I swallowed the smoke. Smoke came out of my nose, and it burned. I coughed.
"You ain't doing it right."
"Here Latrice. You try it."
Latrice pulled from the cigarette, and swallowed the smoke. Smoke came out of her nose, but she didn't cough.
"Can I try it again?"
I wanted to impress Damenia.
"Yeah, you gotta inhale, not swallow the smoke."
I tried again, and inhaled the smoke. Smoke streamed from my nose like a dragon on the attack of his slayer. I thought it was cool.
"Okay, make some smoke rings."
Daminea made a few.
"How do you do that?"
"Open your mouth like this, and push the smoke out with your tongue."
I took another pull and tried to make smoke rings. Latrice took a pull, and we were both unsuccessful. The cigarette burned out and I wanted to make smoke rings. Daminea gave us another cigarette, and before we could light it.
"Kelley, get in the house and eat dinner!"
After dinner, I went back outside and Daminea showed me something else. I coughed so hard I spit up. I was out of my normal mind. I had cotton mouth. I thought people were monsters. It felt like I walked slowly, and everyone watched me. Some friends and I walked to the gas station, and I wanted a pop. I asked for a Sunglo pop and the gas attendant told me they were hot. Maybe I did not hear him, because I asked again, and again. My speech was slurred like a stroke victim.
"Can I have a Slungo pop? Can I have a Slungo Pop? Can I have a Slungo pop?
I spoke very slowly.
"They hot baby. They hot!"
"She high as hell."

The gas attendant new something was wrong with me. I had my first experience with marijuana at nine years old. Daminea or one of the other teenagers told me to drop some visine in my eyes so they wouldn't be so red. I guess Mama would have known if she had seen me. Most of the times, I smoked marijuana, Mama and Daddy were gone. They never found out Daminea gave me marijuana. Daminea was truly the Ringleader, and taught me everything she knew.

Traumatized-3

Loud noises startled me and I awoke to the same as usual; arguments and fights. This time it was the worst I had seen in my nine years of life. I never witnessed a gun being fired before. I never even heard a gunshot until Daddy took his forty five Caliber Revolver and tried to kill David. Daddy had beat Mama again. Something that happened often in our house, but I never observed it. But, this time, David had seen enough. What was to come I didn't quite understand.

"I'm tired of you beating on us."
David was angry.
"Shut the f*ck up."

Daddy grabbed his belt and swung it at David's face. My Daddy was about six inches taller than David. He was a shade less than five feet five inches. However, size did not matter that day. David was determined to not only survive another beating, but to turn the tables on Daddy. David wanted to give Daddy what he had given Mama, Damenia, Chrissy and Allen on too many occasions to remember. Daddy swung his belt and stung a few welts on David's face. David ducked, bobbed, and weaved like a Golden Glove Welterweight champ. He finally found his opening, and caught Daddy's belt in mid-swing with his left hand. David gained control of the belt, and cocked his right fist back, and brought some serious thunder. He cracked Daddy in his mouth so hard all of his teeth flew out of his mouth, all of them; gums and all. That was a new discovery for me. I was unaware of Daddy's false teeth until David exposed them with his blazing right hook. Suffering humiliation from the loss of teeth, and blood at the hands of his son, Daddy angrily walked to his bedroom. David knew what was coming and tried to make like the wind out the front door.
"No D. Don't do it D!"
D was short for Dewitt. Daddy caught David in our living room, and pointed his forty five at David.

"Motherf*cker I will kill you if you ever drawback at me again!"
I didn't know if it was a (scare shot) or a (kill shot), but it was loud and powerful when Daddy fired his gun and missed David's neck by inches. The bullet ripped a hole in the wall, and froze me and everyone into stilled silence. So silent, I could hear the mice and cockroaches crawling between the walls. After the realization of what happened finally thawed us, we screamed and cried. David ran out the front door in his underwear in the dead of winter. Daddy put his gun up, and argued with my Mama about what he had done. I stayed in the living room, and cried until my mind went blank.

My home was already shattered, but after that one unforgettable day, I was traumatized. David (R.I.P) mirrored Daddy. He became an alcoholic who drank Night Train, Wild Irish Rose and forty ounces of Beer with his teenage buddies. When Mama and Daddy were not home, he was very violent. I was afraid of him. I told him if he ever hit me, I would call the police on him. One evening Mama and Daddy weren't home, and David came home drunk. He yelled at me and I ran in the bathroom, and locked the door. David lit some newspaper on fire, and stuck it under the bathroom door. I didn't have any shoes on so I couldn't stomp the fire out. I tried to open the door, but he held the door knob. I turned the water faucet on, and threw water on the fire. It was smoky in the bathroom. I twisted the doorknob, and David was gone. I walked in the kitchen, and he threatened me.

"Put the f*cking phone down before I f*ck you up."
I was so afraid. His eyes were red and he looked really angry. He was a different person when he was drunk. I put the phone down, and ran out of the house. I ran across the street to the pay phone, and called the police. When they arrived, he ran. I told the police what happened, and they told me to go in the house, and don't let him back in until Daddy, and Mama came home. David came home and beat on the door. He begged to come in the house. It was cold outside. I talked to him through the door, and he promised he wouldn't hit me. I let him in, and he staggered right by me, and into his room.

I wanted Mama and Daddy to return soon. I was scared of what he might do to me. I sat on the couch in the living room, and heard him cry in his bedroom. I went in his room to talk to him, and he told me to get out. My heart was filled with pain for David. Mama and Daddy finally came home, and I didn't talk about David because I didn't want him to get in more trouble.

****

The morning after, I learned a valuable life lesson. Mama went upstairs to talk to Peenie and came back down, She told us we were to go fishing with Peenie when the weather was a little better. I was excited. I loved going over to Lake Michigan. Daddy took us there to swim at the beach. I didn't know you could catch fish there. On days it rained, Peenie told us to dig up worms and dirt and put them in a bowl. The lesson I was taught was one of the most positive ones as a child. *Take a man to fish, and you will feed him for a day. Teach a man to fish, and you will feed him for a lifetime.*

Peenie, Nicki, and I walked over to Lake Michigan and began our lifelong lesson. Lake Michigan was a beautiful place. The blue water was calming, and the waves splashed against the shoreline. Seaweeds covered the rocks beneath us, and dead fish floated to the shore of the lake. We sat on the rocks with our feet hanging.

"Okay girls, take one of the worms and connect it to the hook. When you hook it, throw your fishing line into the water. When you notice your line moving, pull back on the rod and reel the line in."
"I got one!"
I stared at the first fish I caught, and wanted to throw him back in. He suffered. He wiggled, and wiggled, but there was no escape.
"Now take the fish off the hook and throw it in the white bucket.

"Ms. Davis, what's the ice for?"
I wasn't allowed to call Peenie by her first name, so I called her Ms. Davis.
"To keep the fish fresh until we get them home."
My hands were dirty with specks of blood on them from the worms. I didn't care. I had fun catching fish.
"Okay, we got a bucket full now let's pack up, and go."
"Mama we home, and we caught a lot of fish."
I didn't know we were going to eat them. Mama had newspaper spread along the entire table. She waited for us.
"Thank you Peenie."
Mama was very grateful.
Peenie kept a few of the fish, but she gave most of them to us.
"Y'all can help me scale the fish."
We scaled the fish, and chopped their heads off. Fish guts were everywhere. Mama did it with pride. She froze some, and deep fried the others. They were delicious; fried perch caught by my little hands. Mama was proud of us. Later on that evening, I was traumatized again. Peenie went to a farm not far from us, and brought some live chickens home. They were running around our courtyard like it was a farm. We chased them.
"Hold 'em."
Peenie was a tough lady. She chopped the head right off the chicken. I had never seen that in my life. I wanted to do it, but it was more gross that chopping the head off of a fish. The chickens ran around with no head. That scared the hell right out of me.

How did any living creature continue to move around without a head? I thought.

The courtyard was painted with bright red blood, headless chickens and guts. I was grossed out. I enjoyed fishing, but there was no way I was going to chop the head off of a chicken. That was just as violent as Daddy firing that gun at David.

****

Kelley Porter

It was a beautiful morning. The birds were chirping, breakfast was ready and I did not pee in the bed. The house was nice, and quiet. I put on my white pants, pink shirt, and gym shoes. I ate breakfast, and headed out to school. I walked East on Fortieth Street to Cottage Grove, and turned right. I walked four blocks to school. I crossed the street at forty third and Cottage Grove, and wanted to stop at Martin Luther King Library, but I didn't have time. I was so proud of myself; no pissy smell. However, the other kids would definitely have something to smell. I saw something on the ground and picked it up. I walked a little faster so I wouldn't be late for school. I approached Forty Fourth Street and made a left onto Evans Street. I was eleven years-old and in the sixth grade. Ms. Martin was my teacher. She was white, and tall with long, brown, shabby hair that was never curled. She dressed like an old lady, but she was probably in her early thirties. She usually wore long skirts, and shirts that were baggy, and not attractive at all. Ms. Martin was soft spoken, nice, and very compassionate.
"Good morning class."
"Good morning Ms. Martin."
"Pass your homework to the student sitting in front of you."
Kelley will you collect the homework, and pass this assignment to your classmates?"
I was the teacher's pet, and always had my way.
"Ms. Martin, can I go to the bathroom?"
"Sure Kelley."
I walked out of the classroom, and into the bathroom. The word
"GIRLS" posted on the door didn't matter because some of the boys tried to come in. I looked under each stall to make sure I was alone. I struck my match, and smoked. I smoked until the bathroom was cloudy. I finished and flushed it down the toilet. On my way out, the eighth graders came in for their bathroom break.
"Man, somebody smoked some good stuff."
One of the eighth graders sniffed in the air.

I walked pass them and out of the bathroom. I went back into my classroom and sat down. A few minutes later, my head hurt.
"Are you okay Kelley?"
"I have a headache."
"Well lay your head down."
Class Dismissed.

"Mama, I got a headache so I'm going to lie down."
"Okay baby."
I woke up hours later from my drug induced sleep, and there were so many people outside.
"Mama, I met a girl named Kathy in school today, and she was very nice. Can I go outside?"
"Sure, baby go ahead."
I went outside, played hopscotch and four corners with some friends.
"Mama, where y'all going? Can I go?"
"Naw, we will be back."
I didn't ask Daddy.
"Latrice, wanna come in and play with me?"
Latrice came in and we went into my bedroom and started freaking. She rolled on my body and sucked my breast. There was no one there to stop us. We smoked a cigarette in the bathroom. We had to stand on top of the bathtub in order to blow the smoke out the window. Latrice heard her mother call her, and had to leave. I watched television until Mama and Daddy came home.
"Baby girl, you wanna go to the store with me?"
"Yeah."
"Don't be anything like Damenia and Chrissy. Go to college, and don't have any kids until you're married. You're smart, and pretty, and you gon' be something in life. You're a go-getter and don't wait around for a man. Be independent. Get a good job, and take care of yourself. I love you Kelley."
"I love you too Daddy."

Daddy always told me he loved me and I believed him despite the fact that he was mean, and didn't buy me many new clothes. Daddy kissed me on the cheek, bought me a blow pop, and some food for the house. I was happy.
"We made it back Mama."
"Go get ready for bed, baby."
I was asleep when Mama came in my room and felt around for a wet spot. Mama was proud of me. She kissed me on the cheek, and said go back to bed. I finally stopped wetting the bed. I remember Mama told me I probably had a weak bladder, so I assumed it was stronger.

I awoke for school, and didn't have any clean clothes to wear. There were no towels, no toothbrush, no soap and, of course no food. My hair was frayed and uncombed. My clothes were dirty. But, I proudly walked to school. I no longer wet the bed.

"You're ants on the rocks."
Katy was one of my classmates. I wasn't sure what she meant, but I walked over to her and tried to send her to the moon. We scratched and pulled each other's hair, and before I could beat her to the ground, her sister jumped in and they both tried to pound me.
"Uh un, both of y'all are not jumping on Kelley!"
Karen was slightly taller than me. She was light-skinned, had a pointed nose, wide-hipped, and wore glasses. She was tough, but very girly. She had long hair, and dressed nicely. We were very good friends in school, and connected instantly. We had several things in common. We both smoked cigarettes, marijuana and played volleyball. Karen jumped in and we fought like cats and dogs. The principal broke the fight up, and I was suspended for three days. I knew that day Karen was my friend, and I could trust her. Later on, she rescued me again.

"Mama, I got into a fight at school, and now I'm suspended for three days."
"What were you fighting about?"

"This girl called me ants on the rocks and I hit her."
"Well, since your ass is suspended you're not going outside."
I went into my room, and was just glad I didn't get a beating.

****

"Kelley you're going with Nippy."
I looked at Damenia with a confused facial expression. I looked at Nippy and he smiled. I had no idea why I was going anywhere with him, nor did I know where. Mama and Daddy weren't home so I had to listen to Damenia. Nippy grabbed my hand, and we walked off.
"I'm sorry for doing what I did, and I want us to be friends."
"Okay."
Sitting on the CTA bus traveling West on thirty-ninth Street, I sat in the seat closest to the window, and Nippy sat next to me. Somehow Nippy convinced Daminea to let me go with him. I knew I wasn't supposed to go anywhere with him, but he apologized and Daminea said it was ok. I stood about four feet nine with one long french braid on each side of my hair. A white barrette dangled from each braid, and touched my shoulder. I wore brown corduroys, a white tee-shirt, and gym-shoes. My feet suspended from the chair about three inches from the ground. I looked out the window, and read the street signs; *Cottage Grove, Prairie, Langley, State, Michigan, King Drive*. Suddenly my attention was taken off of the street signs. I felt his hand on my right thigh and instantly, I was frozen like an ice-sickle. I looked down, and then up only to catch his eyes locked into mine. He smiled, and continued to rub my thigh. I felt very confused. The CTA ride was a very long one. His hand was on my thigh for what felt like eternity. The bus ride finally ended.

On the way home, there was complete silence. We were the only people on the bus who did not say one word. The only people who knew what was going on. His hands moved up to my shoulder, and my hair. I smiled. I thought we were friends. Home at last. I went on to play with my friends as if nothing ever happened. I was traumatized. Mixed emotions crowded my mind like a morning on Wall Street in New York City. But, my mouth never opened again to tell the dark, frightening secrets that I lived with.

Abandoned-4

I grew up in a neighborhood called Oakwood located on the lower end of Chicago. We had four bedrooms, one bathroom, and a half, a large living room, and large closets. Against the wall to the left of the front door, was a brown television-record combo player. A picture with two black people, and two cats shooting dice on velour material hung over the television. To the left of the television, was a black couch with a tear in it that exposed a spring. A long brown cocktail table sat in front of the couch. The kitchen was opposite the couch, and big enough for a table that sat eight people. We didn't have chairs. We had crates. The long hallway housed all four bedrooms.

"Mama, I have volleyball practice today after school so I will make it home around four-thirty."
"Okay, baby. Have fun."

I never thought I would be as good as I was. Mr. Carter was my coach. He was about six feet tall, dark-skinned, medium build, with salt, and pepper hair, and in his late forties or early fifties. He was as strict as Daddy. Carter was there for me, and always encouraged me. He made sure I ate, and got home safely after volleyball games if Daddy didn't pick me up. He had faith in me, and was very nice. He was never mean, but was serious when it came to volleyball. If we didn't follow the rules, Mr. Carter would hit us in the back with a whistle cord. I had my share of hits. Daddy met Mr. Carter when he found out my coach was a man. Surprising enough, Mr. Carter was the only teacher allowed to hit me. I didn't appreciate it, but it paid off in the end. I played volleyball for four years, and my school ranked first place for two years and second place the other two years in the state of Illinois.

The gym room was huge, and all ours. Basketball rims on each end, and a volleyball net right in the center.

"Today I'll teach y'all how to set the ball. Toss the ball in the air, and when it comes down; use the tip of your fingers to push the ball back in the air."

We practiced all day. I did really well. I was so happy. During school, I noticed my neck was swollen and it hurt. I ignored the pain and continued to participate in school. Throughout recess, I wasn't able to turn my neck. The class was almost over, and I was in major pain. I made it home and told Mama. She told me to go lie down. When I awoke, it looked like an apple was stuck to my neck under the skin. I had no idea what it was, but it caused great pain. The slightest touch and I would scream to the top of my lungs.

"Why must you scream like that? Why must you scream like that? Nothing but the dog in you."
Chrissy and David teased me. They laughed, and laughed. I told Mama and Daddy when they got home and they weren't laughing when that extension cord wreaked havoc on them. I wanted to laugh, but it hurt just as well as it did to talk, eat and turn my neck. Mama kept me out of school the next day, and Daddy took me to Michael Reese Hospital, but nothing happened.

We went home and I was miserable. The lump on my neck lasted for what felt like forever. I couldn't practice volleyball anymore. I missed fifty-seven days from school and that included the Iowa test. Some days when the pain wasn't too bad, I went to school and others, I stayed at home. I failed the sixth grade. Daddy never told me what was wrong and why the doctors couldn't fix it. Life just went on with pain and agony for months.

By the summer, that lump finally disappeared. I wasn't able to complete practice over the winter, but I was able to play summer games. Most of the games, I had to sit on the bench because I made too many mistakes. Nevertheless, we came in first place. The start of a new school year, and I was in sixth grade again, and twelve years-old. I wasn't sad, and no one teased me. So I thought nothing of it.

Mr. Christian was my teacher and he was tall, white, plump belly, and had long gray hair. He always wore a ponytail. His blue jeans were always so tight you could see his penis print through his pants. Mr. Christian would yell to the top of his voice if you got on his bad side. He would also kick you out of his classroom if any student misbehaved. I liked Mr. Christian, and once again, I was the teacher's pet.

It was volleyball season and my neck was all better. Last year we came in first place and I received my first trophy. I didn't get to practice much. But, I made up for this year. I practiced hard, and my serve was extremely powerful. We played against Price grammar school located on forty-third and Drexel and slammed them. It was about seven o'clock when I made it home. Mama wasn't home. I took a shower with no soap, and went to bed. Now that I was twelve years old, I awoke, got myself ready for school and ate breakfast. I was able to tell time, so I wasn't going to be late. I was excited about school. I was popular. I was doing excellent in volleyball. My grades were great, and Mr. Christian stopped giving me my spelling test. I guess he knew I would receive one hundred percent so it was unnecessary. When Mr. Christian administered our spelling test, on the last word he always said, *last but not least*. So I decided to mimic him when he asked me to give the spelling test on Fridays.
"And last but not least."

All the students laughed as well as Mr. Christian. I was happy at school. I was so preoccupied with volleyball, my new friend Karen, and helping other students, I didn't see what happened at home. Chrissy and Damenia moved out. Allen and David weren't around much, and Mama was always gone. A lot of the arguing and fighting stopped. It was quiet around the house. Not only was there not a lot of talking, the TV was broken. So I thought.

Our electricity was out for quite some time. Until that one chilling day. It was a Friday night. Nicki and I were in our room talking. We watched our cat Tiger fight with the orange fire flame. She was my seventh birthday gift from Daddy. We named her Tiger since her fur was orange, brown, white, and other colors. Now she was a lot bigger, and wasn't a kitten anymore. She swung at the flame several times. Tiger didn't like fire or water.

"Nicki, get up. The bed is on fire. Nicki wake up!"
Nicki got up and we ran out the room screaming.
"Mama and Daddy the bed is on fire!"
Everybody jumped up in underwear, no shoes, with and without shirts, and ran outside. We had to tell a neighbor to call the fire department. The loud siren made my dog, Killer bark. People were everywhere.
"Everybody back up. Go to the streets. Is it anyone in the house?"
The fireman walked towards the house.
"No. Everybody is out."
Our bedroom was filled with smoke. The fireman walked in with his long hose and put the fire out. It didn't take long for them to extinguish the fire.
"It looks like we found a warm candle under the bed. Keep the windows open until the apartment is completely aired out."

The fireman gave his expert advice and left. Apparently Tiger had another fight with the hot orange flame and won this time. But she started a huge riot. We had to remove the burned and saturated bed out of the room. Now, not only did Nicki and I share the room, we also shared the bed. After that one horrific day, Daddy paid the light bill and we had lights, but the worst was yet to come.

"Daddy, I'm hungry."
"Well, it ain't much, but I made some Chili."
I enjoyed Daddy's chili. We played checkers sometimes to bypass the time. Daddy always won. Mama came home and the explosives began. Daddy didn't hit Mama, but I know his words felt like a blow to the face. I went in my room and closed the door.
"You illiterate, nothing ass motherf*cker!"
"You can kiss my ass Dewitt. I'm sick of this sh*t!"
"F*ck you!"
I fell asleep, and when I awoke, I went into the bathroom, and flicked the light switch up and nothing happened. Daddy wasn't home, and I wasn't sure if he ever came in the night before. Mama made breakfast and a whole lot of noise at the same time. I guess she was mad.

"Baby girl, come and eat breakfast. I gotta go take care of some business."
Mama was angry.
"Okay, Mama is anyone gonna be here when I get out of school?"
"I won't be here, but if your Daddy ain't here, just go to Ms. Baker's or Ms. Davis's house."
"Hey Mama."
Mama was home when I made it from school.
"Hey baby. How do you think you did on the Iowa tests?"
"I know I did good Mama and I'm going to the seventh grade."
"Like I told you, you smart baby."
"What's that thing you using to cook?"
"It's a hotplate baby."
"Is the stove broke?"

"Naw, your Daddy didn't pay the gas bill."
"What are you making for dinner Mama?"
"Neck-bones and rice."
"Well, can I go outside?"
"Yeah, go ahead. I'll call you when dinner is ready."

The courtyard wasn't as pleasant as the earlier years. The swings were broken and hopscotch and four corners disappeared. There was a lot more fighting among the grownups, and teenagers. Families fought families. The garden that used to be filled with tomatoes, cabbage, and greens was covered in mud. Some of my neighbors moved. Mama was absent a lot. Ms. Davis moved so I couldn't fish anymore. Everybody moved out except Nicki. Things had drastically changed over the years. The one thing that changed for the better was Mama and Daddy gave me a little more freedom.

I still had to be in before the street lights came on, but I was able to go a little further away from the house. It was nice not to see Nippy's ugly face again, and I didn't have to worry about performing sexual acts for Daminea. Life was depressing in and out of the house, and I thought it couldn't get any worse. I went in the house, and noticed Mama had left her cigarettes on the cocktail table and went into the bathroom. I stared at them and debated if I should take one, and would I get caught. It wasn't the first time I stole cigarettes from Mama. I got the idea from Latrice. I walked over to the cocktail table and took two cigarettes out of her pack and wasn't sure where to hide them. I didn't want them to break. By the time I figured out where I would hide them, Mama walked in the living room. I didn't know she was coming since she always left the bathroom door open when no one was home.

"What the hell are you doing?"
"Nothing."
"Open your hands!"

I opened my hands, and Mama punched me right in the arm. I dropped the cigarettes.

"You stealing from me and you're smoking! I'm 'bout to beat your ass!"

Mama got the extension cord, and more welts covered my body.

"Mama, that hurt."

"Didn't I tell your ass not to be smoking?"

Screams echoed through the apartment.

"Shut up!"

I screamed, jumped, twisted, and turned.

"Be your ass still and don't you ever steal from me again and nobody else for that matter! Now shut your ass up and go to your room."

****

School started and I was thirteen years-old, and in the seventh grade. Ms. Cervantes was my teacher. She was white, tall and slim with short brown hair. She always wore black slacks that looked dingy, and her black shoes were run down. Ms. Cervantes was stern. She demanded respect, and didn't tolerate any mess from any student. She wasn't too quick to hit a student, but she would definitely embarrass or send you to the principal's office. Ms. Cervantes had no problem calling a student out of their name. I never had that problem because I was afraid of her until I earned my position as teacher's pet. Ms. Cervantes took a liking to me because I was very intelligent, and exhibited excellent behavior.

"Kelley, will you come here for a second?"

I walked to Ms. Cervantes's desk, and she asked me to tutor one of the students in my classroom. I actually felt sorry for this particular classmate because the students teased her. She wasn't illiterate, but she had difficulties understanding the work. I was grateful Ms. Cervantes thought that much of me to ask me to tutor her. I knew I did well in school, but that meant I would be taken away from my own work. Ms. Cervantes had enough confidence in me to know that it wouldn't be a problem for me to catch up. I tutored my classmate in Language Arts and Math. I tutored her for a few months, and on occasion I tested her and reported back to Ms. Cervantes. Sometimes it was frustrating because I didn't know the extent of her learning disability. Ms. Cervantes actually cared about whether or not we did well. *The bell rang for dismissal.*

"Does anybody know where Janie lives?"
A man approached our building looking for Mama.
"That's my Mama."
"Can you go get her for me?"
"Mama, it's a man out here for you."
I was confused.
Mama didn't respond. I walked away from our front door, and Mama came out with a brown suitcase in her hand.
"Mama, are you coming back?"
I honestly don't recall if she said yes or no.
"Bert this is my daughter Kelley."
"Hi."
Bert was Mama's new boyfriend. He didn't talk a lot, nor did he smile a lot. I really didn't know much about him other than he was the man who took my mother away. Mama hugged, kissed me on the cheek, got in the car with Bert, and drove off. I watched the car as it drove away and became invisible.
"Daddy, where did Mama go?"
"I don't know."
"Is she coming back?"
"I don't know."

On the way to Kentucky Fried Chicken, Daddy and I talked about what would happen if Mama didn't come back home. Daddy told me I would have to live with Chrissy. We went to the Checkerboard lounge across the street, and I watched Daddy shoot a few pool games. On the way home, we stopped at the store to pick up a few things. We made it home and I washed a few outfits for school. Daddy and I watched TV for the rest of the evening until it was time for me to go to bed. I cried myself to sleep because I missed Mama. I hadn't talked to her in about a month. I wanted Mama. I needed her. Life was really hard. Daddy had become Mama. He cooked for me and dropped me off at school sometimes. He was home more than before.

"What's wrong Daddy?"

"Kelley, I can't take care of you no more. I'll have to let you go live with Chrissy."

"Daddy, please I don't wanna live with Chrissy. I wanna stay with you. Please Daddy."

"Well, we can't stay here no more. So pack up your clothes, and we're leaving today."

I was happy Daddy said I could continue living with him. I didn't care where we lived. I just didn't want to live with Chrissy. I wondered where Mama was. She still hadn't called or stopped by. Daddy took me to an apartment building where we stayed for the weekend. There were quite a few older men and women that lived in the building. We had one room and a kitchen. There was a bathroom in the corridors of each floor, and it was shared by the tenants that lived on that level.

"Kelley, it's too many old men here and I don't want you living around them. I don't want you sharing the bathroom with them. I don't want nothing to happen to you so I'll take you to Chrissy's house."

I cried and cried.

"Can we go and stay somewhere else then? Why can't I stay with you? Can you find us an apartment? Daddy, please."

My eyes were bloodshot, and mucus drooled from my nose. I cried as we drove from the low end to my new place of residence. I never wanted to live with any relative other than my parents. I was thirteen years old, and the worst thing ever happened to me, I was abandoned by Mama and Daddy.

"Hey Chrissy. I'll need you to take care of Kelley."
"Daddy, will you come get me on weekends?"
"Yeah baby."
"Bye Daddy."

I gave Daddy a big hug and kiss and off he went. Daminea, Nicki and David were living there, and I was happy to see them. Chrissy told me to put my clothes in the dining room because that's where I would sleep. I went in the living room to watch TV and heard keys at the door so I looked up, and it was him. Nippy walked in. I asked why he had keys and found out he lived there. I laid on the floor and watched The *Jeffersons*.
"Your booty got big."

I didn't breathe a word because I remembered when I was blamed for what he did before. I ignored him, and continued to watch TV. Night fell and it was time for bed. I slept in the dining room right next to the kitchen. The apartment had one bedroom, with an enclosed front porch, a living room, dining room, and kitchen.

Time went by and still no word from Mama. Living in Chrissy's place was worse than living at home. The verbal violence, no food and extremely violent fights were like nothing I ever witnessed. The abuse I witnessed and experienced at Chrissy's house was far more terrible than the abuse Daminea inflicted upon me at home with Mama and Daddy. It was torture, and my heart was filled with pain and anger.

Daddy picked me up from Chrissy's place and took me out to eat and buy clothes. I saw him on the weekends on a regular. I needed to see him. We went to Daley's restaurant on sixty-third Street and had dinner. Sometimes we drove down to Prairie Shores to eat soup. I really enjoyed being with Daddy. I missed Mama so much. Months went by and still no word from her.

Chrissy struggled to care for me, and she wanted Daddy to turn over part of his Social Security check so she could care for me. After Daddy gave her his money, I didn't see him as much. Daddy gave me about three hundred dollars a month. The money was supposed to be used for my clothing, food, and bus-fare for school. Although I made it to school, there weren't many new clothes or food for that matter. Chrissy forced me to pay rent at thirteen years old, and I was upset. We argued all the time because I knew I was not supposed to pay rent. Daddy gave me that money to care for myself, but Chrissy thought otherwise. Chrissy, Daminea, Kenneth and Nippy were all on drugs, and that's what my money was used for.

Kenneth was Chrissy's boyfriend, and he was tall, dark and handsome. He had a slim build with an Afro that was usually permed or texturized. He was well-groomed, but had a dark side that was dangerous, insecure, abusive, mean, and just downright ugly. He was one crazy man. Many days we had grits and cheese for breakfast or no food at all. Nippy gave me money to buy food from the restaurant, and always told me not to tell anyone. So I didn't. Not even a month after living there, Damenia introduced me to cocaine.

"Sniff this Kelley."
"What is it?"
"Cocaine."
"Stick your finger in it, and put it to your nose, and sniff it."

I did what Daminea told me to do, and it felt like I walked on air. I didn't like the feeling, so I laid down. Days in that house of getting high were like time, it never stopped. After Mama beat me for smoking cigarettes, I quit. After I moved in with Chrissy, I started smoking cigarettes and marijuana again. Daminea gave me cocaine again, and I really didn't want to do it, but I had to listen to her.

Night fell and it was time for me to go to bed. Nicki and I slept on opposite sides of the dining room. We slept right next to the kitchen where the water bugs and rats lived. I could hear them eating, among other things. I looked to my right, and Nippy moved up and down on Nicki. I didn't know what to think so I never said anything. I laid there, watched and listened. I thought it was okay. Nicki did it and I wanted to do what Nicki did. Many nights I watched Nippy having sex with Nicki and no one ever knew. I never said a word to Nicki that I knew of her secret. I went on as if nothing ever happened. Chrissy, Daminea and Kenneth were too busy smoking crack, and they never knew what went on. I wondered if they cared. Eventually that was all they did. Daily, they were locked up in the bedroom smoking crack. I hung out in the game room playing Pac-man, Millipede, Centipede, Galaxy, and other games.

In the game room, I met a man who was twice my age. He liked me, and wanted to meet my cousins. I don't remember his name, but I do remember the outcome.

"Who are you?"

"I like Kelley."

"Well, you too motherf*cking old for her and you better leave her alone."

He left and never bothered me again, but what was to come was worse than ever.

Perfectly Planned — (Overcoming Incest, Rape & Sexual Abuse)

Chester the Molester -5

Easter 1984
"Kelley, take your clothes off."
Nippy came in the dining room and this time he didn't bother Nicki.
"It hurt. Stop."
"Okay, let me try again."
"No. Stop."

Eventually he stopped and I was clueless to what had happened. The next morning there was blood in my underwear. I didn't know how to tell. Time went on and so did life. Nippy continuously came into the dining room in the middle of the night and had sex with me. He would stick his d*ck in me and move up and down on me as he did Nicki and Daminea. I thought it was the thing to do. I saw him do it to Nicki and no one said a word so I thought it was acceptable.

The next evening, David came home drunk and started an argument with Chrissy for whatever reason. They fought and Chrissy threw punches like Muhammad Ali. She and David threw blows at each other like they were two men fighting on the streets. I cried and screamed. I wanted them to stop. I wanted somebody to break the fight up. I hated the violence. It made me want to vomit. Kenneth came home and broke the fight up and stood right between Chrissy and David. David knocked Chrissy right in her eye and it began to swell and turn black and blue right before my eyes. I was so sad for her. David walked away and Kenneth went after him. David tried to run and Kenneth pushed him right off our third floor balcony. We screamed. My cousins ran to the back porch to look and see if David was down there. I knew at that moment he was dead this time.

"Where is he? He ain't down there."

We all cried hysterically. My cousins ran downstairs and I walked to the back and looked off the balcony and was relieved that I didn't see David lying there in a pool of blood. He had somehow miraculously landed on the second floor balcony. He was like an acrobat that soared through the air to their partner. He never hit the ground. Although he was very violent, I didn't want him to die. David left and the house was quiet for a while. I hated Kenneth that day. I hated Kenneth and David for all the pain they caused.

****

It was my last days of seventh grade. I was thirteen years old and looking forward to the summer. *The bell rang for dismissal.* I passed to the eighth grade and was excited. When I got home, Chrissy, Daminea, Nippy and Kenneth were there. Chrissy and Daminea were cooking dinner and I had to clean up. After I was done cleaning, I went in the living room to watch TV. The TV was positioned right next to the hallway leading to the kitchen. I laid on the floor and watched *Different Strokes*.

"Give me a tongue kiss."
Nippy touched my butt.
"I don't know how."
"Stick your tongue back and forth in my mouth."
"Now pull your pants down and bend over and pretend like you're turning the channel on the TV. Make sure don't nobody come down the hallway."
Nippy had sex with me in the living room while my cousins were twenty feet away and told me not to tell Daminea because he would just beat her ass and she would beat mine. The next morning I got up and took a shower.
"Chrissy what is this white stuff in my underwear?"
"It's discharge and it's normal."
"Okay."

After dinner I went to bed and was awakened by noises. Nippy was on top of Nicki again. I laid there and watched. Nippy looked over at me and smiled. I pretended like I was asleep. When he was done he walked back into the living room and went to sleep. The next day while I was standing outside in front of the building, I saw the same car pull up that drove Mama away.

"Mama!"
I ran over and gave her a big hug.
"Is that a black eye? Did he hit you?"
Chrissy was angry.
"Naw. Bert didn't hit me."
Mama was not convincing at all.
"She ran into a doorknob."
"If I find out you hitting her I'll f*ck you up!"
Mama came upstairs for a little while, but Bert was ready to go.
"Mama, can I come live with you?"
"I'll have to talk to Bert. Write my phone number down."
I wrote Mama's number down and called her the next day.
"Mama, can I come live with you?"
"Let me ask Bert. Baby Bert said no."
"Why? I don't wanna live with Chrissy. I wanna come live with you." I cried.
"I'm sorry baby. I'll talk to you later."
"Bye Mama."

Mama was gone again. Volleyball ended and I had nothing to show for it. Little gold statues with a ball in one hand and the other hand held high with the palm open. I was proud until my gold statue clocked David up aside his head.
"You ain't gon' keep bringing your drunken ass in here starting fights!"

They went at it like cats and dogs. I was scared of her and David. Chrissy grabbed my trophy off the fireplace and knocked David dead in the head. One gold statue down, three to go. I thought David would go down, but the alcohol kept him going. I thought they were going to kill each other. Once again, I wanted to vomit. My stomach turned into knots and I was broken hearted to see my family beat each other like animals. But, Chrissy had to defend herself. The brawl ended when we called the police. David was told to get out of the house and not come back.

****

The summer ended and I was fourteen. There wasn't anything exciting for me to do after volleyball. The most excitement was fighting inside and out. I hated all of it. I didn't see Mama again for about a year.
"Kelley, come here."
"Take your clothes off and lie on the couch."
"What the f*ck!"
Daminea awoke. In the middle of the night Nippy awoke me and took me into the living room. I laid on the couch with no clothes on and he had sex with me. Motionless and confused with a blank stare on my face, Nippy bumped Daminea's arm and she awoke.
"Chrissy Kelley in here f*cking Nippy!"
I got up, pulled my clothes up and just stood there. Nippy smiled and waited for Chrissy to awake. He always said he was going to get me. I just didn't know what he meant.
"What the f*ck is going on?"
"I just caught Kelley f*cking Nippy."
"What!"
Chrissy punched me in the face then Daminea punched me in the face. I cried. I didn't know what to do. I was scared.

"B*tch get the f*ck out with your nasty ass! Trifling motherf*cker, nasty ass f*cking your cousin's man! You ain't gon' be sh*t! Nasty motherf*cker. What the f*ck is wrong with you? Get the f*ck out! B*tch don't cry now. You wasn't crying when you was f*cking him was you? Stupid ass. Your ass gon' be lost and turned out. Nippy you got to get the f*ck out my house!"

Nippy left and Chrissy put me out of her house. I was fourteen years old. Neither Mama nor Daddy had been around in a while. Chrissy closed the door and I sat in the hallway and cried. I didn't have anywhere to go.

"Bring your stupid ass back in the house. You sitting there with that dumb ass look on your face. I ought to f*ck you up!"
"Just leave her alone and let's go back to bed."

Kenneth stopped Chrissy from beating me up anymore. I never exposed Nicki's secret because after what happened to me, I didn't want her to get in trouble. In the morning, Nicki decided to tell Chrissy about her and Nippy. Chrissy called the police to make a report on Nippy. Daminea tried to hit Nicki in the head with a stick. Daminea was very angry and she beat me up again. No one intervened. I just stood there being beat up. I never wanted to fight so I didn't try to fight back.
"You nasty ass b*tch."
Punch after punch.
"Your ass aint sh*t and aint gon' never be sh*t. You trifling ass whore!"
I cried and cried. I wanted Mama and Daddy. I wanted to die. I went into the bathroom and took some pills. I wasn't sure what they were. I left the house and ran until I couldn't run anymore. No one knew where I was. I ran over to the lake and my first mind told me to jump in. I was able to swim, but not in Lake Michigan and I knew if I jumped I wouldn't make it out alive.
"Kelley what are you doing?"
Kenneth followed me.
"Leave me alone."
"Come here Kelley. It's gon' be okay. I'm taking you home."

Kenneth grabbed me.

"I don't wanna go back there because they gon' keep beating me up." I cried.

"Nobody's gonna touch you again."

We walked back to the house and Chrissy noticed a medicine bottle open in the bathroom.

"Did you take some pills? Why yo' stupid ass wanna die?" The police arrived and they told Chrissy and Daminea that they would place a warrant out for Nippy's arrest. His real name was Tyrone Brown Sr. He was wanted for Statutory Rape. The officers also told Chrissy to get counseling for me. It never happened.

****

School started and I was in the eighth grade. Mr. Alexander was my teacher and he was tall, dark, and handsome with a medium build and a low haircut. He always dressed in a nice dark colored suit with a tie. Mr. Alexander was a no nonsense type of man. He had a nice bubbly personality and was always in a good mood. He believed in making us students do the best we could. Mr. Alexander had a lot of faith in us. After just a month in class, Mr. Alexander wanted me to tutor the second and third grade students in Math, but this time it was after school and I got paid for it. It wasn't much, but I earned it. In addition, this year my school developed a Class Government. I was selected to run for president and my opponent was Carlos Marshall. We both prepared a speech and then read it over the intercom system.

Carlos Marshall was my enemy. We competed in a Spelling test in the sixth grade and he won. Carlos was not too taller than me, dark skin and always had something bad to say about me. He played entirely too much and I didn't like him. After weeks of preparing my speech, I was ready. I presented my speech and so did Carlos. After all the votes were in, Carlos Marshall won the president's seat and I won the vice president's seat. I wasn't disappointed at all. I was just happy to win this time. After working with Carlos Marshall as his Vice President, we developed a friendship and learned to be friends.

After school I hoped Daddy would pick me up and take me away. My wish didn't come true. I caught the bus home and as soon as I walked up to our building. Everybody stared at me.
"She fucked her cousin's man."
Damenia and one of our neighbors were outside talking.
"Both of their nasty asses."
"Kelley why did you do that?"
I never answered. I just walked into the building.
"Because the b*tch nasty and gon' be lost and turned out."
Every day was filled with tears, name calling and beatings. Chrissy,
Daminea and Kenneth continued to smoke crack and I barely ate. Every day I wanted to die in that house. The only place I felt good about myself was at school. Everybody liked me there. I was popular, very intelligent, and competed in spelling and math competitions. I tutored students and received payment and was the vice president of the Student Council. But, most of all, I assisted our volleyball team to rank second place in the State of Illinois.

Graduation was approaching and I hoped Mama and Daddy would be there. I really missed her. I knew I was going to the ninth grade and since Hyde Park was not far from me, I would attend there for high school. I called Mama and Daddy a few days before graduation and they told me they would be there and this time they didn't let me down.
"Mama! Hey Mama!"

I gave her a big hug.
"Hey Bert." I frowned.
"How are you doing Kelley?"
"Fine."
I didn't want him there. I didn't like him at all.
"Daddy!"
I gave him a big hug. Mama and Daddy didn't talk much to each other.
"I'm proud of you baby."
"Thanks Mama."
This was one of my best days. Mama and Daddy were right by my side.
"Kelley Porter!"
Dr. Taylor was the principal at our school. I proudly walked across the stage and accepted my Grammar school diploma. Mama and Daddy gave me a big hug. I was so happy and wanted to be with them, but that was impossible. Mama did not want to be around Daddy.
"I'm proud of you baby and I love you. I gotta go and I will see you later."
"Okay Daddy."
Mama and Bert took me out to eat and then back to Chrissy's house. They didn't stay long because Bert was ready to go. I enjoyed my time spent with Mama and Daddy. I knew it would be a while before I saw her again.

Back at the house, Nippy hung around so that he could see Daminea. Chrissy didn't want him in our house anymore. I didn't hate him. I didn't know how I was supposed to feel. I wanted to be around him. He told me Chrissy and Daminea didn't love me and that he was the only one that did. Nippy also told me that they would always beat me. I believed him. I thought he was telling me the truth. He said he was my friend. I trusted him. He didn't beat or belittle me and I didn't want him to go to jail.
"All rise!"

Chrissy, Daminea and I were at Nippy's trial for the crime he committed against me. I looked behind me and Nippy sat on the opposite side of the courtroom smiling. I smiled back.

"Tyrone Brown Sr., you have been found guilty of Statutory Rape against a minor child. You will serve two years' probation. If you break any laws during this time you will serve two years in prison."

That didn't stop Nippy from hanging around. Daminea and Chrissy were missing in action and he brought me money and cigarettes. I used the money to buy food. Food was sparse around our house because Daminea and Chrissy were too busy smoking crack. Life was at an all-time low for me. Mama and Daddy were never around. There was always bloodshed at Chrissy house. I was always criticized. The normal language in our house was b*tch this, whore that, dumb ass, slut, lost and turned out, trifling ass motherf*cker stupid ass, you aint gon' be sh*t. I heard all of these words directed at me. They made me feel worthless. If I had a gun I would've blown my head off. I wished I would have fallen asleep and never awakened.

But I did on the first day of school at Hyde Park Career Academy, located at sixty two twenty South Stony Island. I was fifteen years old and a freshman. My homeroom teacher was Ms. Murphy. She was kind of tall, overweight, and dark-skinned with short hair. Mrs. Murphy was stern, yet nice. She dressed fashionably and had a good sense of humor. After taking attendance, she would talk to us about what was going on in school and how we were doing. She sometimes cracked a joke or two.

On the first day I met a girl named Lonita Mondane Hicks and we became good friends. I remained happy on the outside, but felt like I was dying on the inside. No-one loved me, but Nippy. Damenia and Chrissy hated me and Mama and Daddy didn't care. I was totally confused about what sex I liked. I thought girls and boys were pretty. I wanted to be with girls sexually as well as boys. I felt like an outcast at school. I felt like a bum, but I held my head up high. I didn't have nice clothes and my hair was never pretty. But, I remembered what Mama told me. *Don't worry about what people say about you. Go to school to learn and get a good education.* I held on to that. That was all I had. Every day during lunch period I never had any lunch money and was too embarrassed to go into the lunchroom. Lonita bought me French fries sometimes from the food truck that parked in front of our school. She was really nice to me. She gave me clothing, fed me and helped with my school work. I maintained B's and C's. I never attended a basketball, football or baseball game and I didn't join the volleyball team. My first few months in high school were nothing more than a freak show at my expense.

Look at those clothes she got on. She got an elastic waistline. Look at her hair. Some of the other students teased me. I never responded to any of the negative remarks. I just kept my head up and continued on. After school, I went home and there was no food and I wanted to stay home, but I was hungry. I did my homework and walked to the gas station to meet Nippy. He was waiting in a brown car. No-one ever paid attention other than to pound on or criticize me. He bought me some Burger King and we drove to the Lake on sixty third and Lake Shore Drive.

"Sniff this Kelley."
"Okay."
"Now take your pants off and open your legs."
"What you do that for?"
"It's gonna feel real good."

Nippy had sex with me in the back of his car and I laid there motionless with a blank stare on my face.
"Move your hips."
"Huh."
"You gotta roll your body. That's good."
"What's that white stuff that came out of me?"
"That's nut."
"What's nut?"
"Sperm. It's how a man gets a woman pregnant."
"I don't wanna get pregnant."
"Okay. I won't do it again."
"What was that you put down there?"
"The same thing you sniffed."
"Cocaine, why did you do that?"
"Because it numbs your p*ssy and it won't hurt and I can f*ck longer. But I don't want you sniffing this stuff anymore; okay. It ain't good for you. Damenia should have never given it to you. I told you she don't love you. I'm the only one that loves you."
"Okay."

Nippy took me back to the gas station and I walked home. No one ever asked where I have been, if I was hungry or if my homework was done. Not one concern. They were too busy getting high. I never sniffed cocaine again, but I met Nippy numerous times at the gas station. It was always the same thing.

One day Daminea followed me and she told Chrissy I was going to meet Nippy. When I made it home they were all waiting for me.
"Where the f*ck you been?"
"Outside."
"Where outside? Did you go meet Nippy and b*tch don't lie? I'll knock the f*ck out of you if you lie to me!"
"I saw Phil and got a cigarette from him."
I was very nervous. Phil was Nippy's cousin and the brown car belonged to him.

"B*tch you're lying. Daminea said she saw you meet up with Nippy at the gas station. Don't get quiet now. I oughta knock the sh*t out of you with your stupid ass. You ain't got no business f*cking with Damenia's man. What the f*ck you thinking about? You ain't listening to me. You f*cking nasty. If I catch you with him I'll beat your ass. Now get the f*ck out my face you nasty, trifling ass motherf*cker!"

I laid on my bed and cried myself to sleep. I knew I had met Nippy, but why would I tell. They would just beat me again. I kept my mouth shut. I really didn't know what to do. Nippy always said it was right and my family didn't love me. I visualized how I could die. I didn't want to live anymore. My life wasn't worth it.

I met with Nippy after school and told him to leave me alone. He wouldn't. I was too scared to tell Chrissy. She didn't love me. She only wanted to hurt me. I couldn't tell Mama and Daddy because they didn't want me. Nippy always told me they didn't love me and he was the only one that did. I believed him. My home was so depressing. Almost every day, Damenia called me a stupid trifling ass b*tch; nasty or lost and turned out. I believed her and Chrissy. I believed my life was not worth living. Death was my only way out. Night fell and those same thoughts. *I hope I don't wake up, I want to die, and maybe I can stab myself in the stomach. Will it hurt too badly? Will I be able to stick the knife all the way in? Maybe I should walk in front of a moving car. I just don't want to wake up.*

My alarm went off and I had to wake up. I really didn't want to. I dreamt about being with a girl. There wasn't any breakfast so I left early and went over to Lonita's house so that I could eat breakfast. Lonita was short, fair-skinned, medium build, very smart and always dressed nicely. She was a kind friend and always helped me in any way I needed.

Lonita lived in a town house with her mother and step-father. I liked her family. She had a nice family and none of them used drugs. They were all professional women with houses and husbands. In Lonita's house it was very quiet and peaceful. Her family treated me like I was one of them. They were very positive people and always wanted to help me. I knocked on Lonita's door.
"Who is it?"
"Kelley."
"It's my friend Kelley Mama."
"Okay, let her in."
"Hey Ms. Hicks. Hey Lonita."
"Good Morning Kelley."
Ms. Hicks was always so kind to me.
"Hey girl. You're here early."
"I know. I just wanted to get out of that house."
"Your cousins shouldn't be calling you a b*tch. That's just disrespectful."
"I know. But, that's how they talk to me."
"Well are you hungry?"
"Yep."
"Do you want some cereal?"
"Yeah."
"Well, you know where the bowls are. Help yourself."
"I had a dream about being with a girl last-night. What do you think about being with girls?"
"Well, that's not right and I don't like that."
At that point I never talked about lesbianism with Lonita again because it was off limits.
"Are you ready Kelley?"
"Yep. Thanks for the cereal."
Now I don't have to go to school hungry. I thought.
Lonita and I talked and laughed on our way to school. It was a good morning.
Class dismissed.
I saw Phil's car parked across the street. Nippy beckoned me and I walked over.
"Get in. I wanna take you somewhere."

Nippy unlocked the door. He did a U-turn and we drove South on Stony Island. We pulled into a lot and he parked the car.
"What is this place?"
"Just wait a minute."
Nippy got out of the car.
"Can I go in?"
"Naw. They don't need to see you. Wait here."
"Come on."
"Is this what you call a hotel?"
I looked around.
"Something like it. It's a motel"
Nippy undressed himself.
"What's the difference?"
"I don't really know."
Nippy laid naked on the bed.
"Come here."
Smoke filled the room and felt like it was spinning.
"Chrissy said this is wrong Nippy."
I fanned the smoke away from my face.
"Well, she just jealous and mad 'cause I don't want her. I love you Kelley and you said you love me. They don't love you. If they did, do you think they would treat you like sh*t and beat you up. You can't tell nobody cause they gon' beat your ass again. Now come here and take your clothes off."
"Are you hungry?"
Nippy cleaned himself.
"Yeah. Why you keep putting this nut in me? I thought you said it's for getting a woman pregnant. I don't wanna get pregnant."
"It is. So you gotta do the calendar method."
"What's that?"
"Keeping up with your period. Your period comes once a month and two weeks after you can get pregnant. When we have sex I will just withdraw."
"What's that?"
"Right before I nut, I'll pull it out so that it don't go in you. Do you want some rib tips?"
Nippy dressed himself.

"Yeah, and I wanna go."
I jumped off the bed.
"Just stay here until I come back."
"How come I can't go?"
Cus I ain't supposed to be messing with you and if the police see us together, I can go to jail."
"Why you gon' go to jail?"
"Remember when we went to court and they said I was not supposed to be around you or I will go to jail?"
"Yeah."
"Well, that's it. So come lock the door and I will be right back."
Nippy walked out the door. I didn't understand why Nippy would go to jail. I didn't know what was wrong. All I knew was that he said he loved me and my family didn't. I really didn't understand. I was scared since I had never been in a hotel before. I saw matches on the table that read Zanzibar motel so I lit a cigarette and smoked it. I was high and paranoid. After a while, I forgot I was alone until I heard keys at the door. Nippy came back with rib tips, chicken and French fries. After we were done eating, Nippy dropped me off around the corner from Chrissy's house.
"Don't tell Damenia where you been or she gon' beat your ass."
"Okay."
It was late in the evening when I returned home and no one noticed. Kenneth answered the door and walked back into his room with Chrissy. He and Chrissy was getting high again and I didn't know where Daminea was. I went into the dining room to do my homework and Chrissy and Kenneth came out of their bedroom. They didn't say much to me. Nicki came home and we started singing and dancing. Nicki recorded music from the radio station WGCI and she taught me. We always recorded music together. She taught me to do a few other things such as how to sew my pants, swim, French braid my hair, and a whole lot more. I really trusted Nicki, although we had our arguments and fights, she always treated me like family. Except that one time, she slapped me because I accidentally tore her Duran Duran poster. We fought and I tried to bite her face off.

I didn't understand how someone could get so angry over a poster and become violent.

After school Nippy was outside waiting again.
"Who is that Kelley?"
"My friend."
"He looks too old for you."
Lonita looked over at Nippy.
"Well, I gotta go. See you tomorrow."
I walked toward Nippy's car.
"Hey Nippy. What you doing up here again?"
"We're going to our special place again."
"Oh. I'm hungry."
I rubbed my stomach. Nippy did a U-turn and drove South on Stony Island. We drove to the Zanzibar hotel. Nippy didn't want me to get out of the car. He always wanted me to wait in the car. I didn't see the big deal. But, I just waited. Nippy walked to the front office, but this time he didn't retrieve a key.
"We gotta go to another hotel. They don't have any rooms left."
"What happened to all their rooms?"
"Well, it's Friday and a lot of people like to get rooms on the weekends. So weekends are really busy for hotels."
"Oh."
"So we gon' go to the one down the street."
Nippy drove further South on Stony Island and we pulled into a hotel called the Seville motel.
"Wait here."
Nippy exited the car. I smoked a cigarette and waited. Nippy walked back to the car and drove around to the back of the building. Our room was on the first floor and it wasn't as clean as the Zanzibar.
"We got eight hours."
"What does that mean?"
"Well, you can pay for four, eight hours or all night and that gives me more time."
"Oh."
"Roll that up for me."

Nippy gave me a brown bag of marijuana and some tops. I rolled up a joint and lit it.
"Gimme me a shotgun. Don't burn your mouth."
I stuck the lit end of the joint in my mouth and blew smoke in his and he started coughing. I laughed and laughed while he coughed and coughed. His cough was so loud and strong, it sounded like he had the Whooping cough.
"Yo' turn."
I inhaled the smoke and pulled away from his mouth because the smoke was too strong. I coughed, but not as hard as Nippy.
"Roll another one."
I rolled another joint and smoked it until I passed out. I woke up with Nippy on top of me. It hurt. He pumped very hard and I wanted him to stop, but he wouldn't. I screamed and finally he made a loud noise and stopped. I grabbed my stomach, rolled over and went to sleep.
"Wake up, it's time to go."
"Keep your mouth closed!"
I went in the house and once again Chrissy, Kenneth and Daminea were getting high. I sat in the dining room and thought about Mama and Daddy. I wanted them to come get me and take me away. My body enjoyed the adult pleasures that Nippy gave me, but I wanted to be with Mama and Daddy. I hated living with Chrissy and Kenneth. They didn't love me. All they cared about was crack. Suicidal thoughts took over my mind.

I want to die. I want to ingest rat poison. I wonder if we have any. Maybe I can stab myself, but it might hurt. I wonder if I leave the house would anybody notice. Maybe I could leave the house and somebody could kidnap and kill me.

My thoughts were interrupted by an argument between Chrissy and Kenneth. I wasn't sure why they argued, but he was very angry. Kenneth went into the bathroom and smashed the mirror with his bare hand. There was blood everywhere. The paramedics had to come get him. When he came home his hand was wrapped in a white cast. I decided to go to bed and hoped I wouldn't awake, but I did to Chrissy's screams.

"Leave me alone Kenneth."

"Kenneth leave Chrissy alone. Leave her alone."

I cried and pushed their bedroom door. The latch was on. I pushed harder. I pushed the door as hard as I could. The door opened and Kenneth's hand move forward and into Chrissy's stomach. Her eyes widened and she grabbed her stomach. Kenneth wrapped his arm around her shoulder and walked her toward the door. I noticed blood on her hand there was a trail of blood from her bedroom to the living room door. The paramedics arrived and took Chrissy away. I was in a state of shock and was oblivious as to what really happened. Chrissy had internal bleeding. I thought her time was over. I cried. I hated Chrissy, but I did not want to lose her. I hated Kenneth more.

What would I do without Chrissy? Who would take care of me? How would I live? What would happen to me? I thought. Chrissy lived. She was very mean to me, but I needed her, I loved her. She was all I had. I wanted to kill Kenneth with my bare hands. I wanted to cleave his heart right out of his chest. Chrissy was in the hospital for a while. Neither Mama nor Daddy came to get me. I was left there with Daminea, Kenneth and David. It didn't last long for the reason that we were evicted. When Chrissy was discharged from the hospital a few months passed and we packed our belongings. I learned later that Nippy lied to Kenneth and told him Chrissy was talking to another man and that's what started the almost deadly fight between Kenneth and Chrissy. Nippy was the reason Kenneth almost killed Chrissy.

We moved to one of the projects located on the lower end of Chicago. I had never seen so many drugs in my life. Almost the entire building flooded with drug addicts, gang bangers and trigger happy thugs. Nippy continuously came around. I don't know how he knew where we lived. I hated Nippy for lying to Kenneth and almost costing Chrissy her life. He would not stay away. Daminea told everybody that I f*cked her man. She and Chrissy condemned me in every neighborhood we moved to.

I started to suppress all the pain and pretend my life was great. I pretended my family's lives were great also. I lied to people whenever they asked how everyone else was doing. *Daminea was a supervisor at McDonalds. Chrissy was a supervisor at the Best Western hotel over housekeeping. Nicki was a police officer. Allen owned his own business and I blocked David out.*

I lived in a fairy tale in my mind. I smiled all the time and always tried to look good. Chrissy, Daminea, Allen, and David were all hooked on drugs. Even though Nicki never became addicted, I hated that she experimented because I was afraid I would lose her too. I had no one to inspire me to do better. My heart ached every day. Drugs were taking my family away from me. Death was coming closer and closer to me every day. No one understood why I was so angry. It hurt so bad to see Chrissy smoking crack or to watch Allen and Daminea nodded out and scratching like bugs invaded their bodies or to find David asleep in the grass. I didn't care how much or how little they used or experimented, I was hurt by it. I was fifteen years old and lived like a complete bum. Our apartment was simply a crack house. It was like a police station; dicks were in and out. I couldn't concentrate living in that house. Chrissy never wanted me there. I hated the drugs. Every morning I washed up at the sink. There were always clothes in the bathtub. There was never any soap. If I had a face towel, David wiped his butt on it and hung it on the towel rack. The one thing that kept me alive was school.

Although I was dying on the inside, I really enjoyed learning. I wasn't doing as well in high school as I did at grammar, but I kept going. Before I could finish freshman year, Chrissy evicted me.

"B*tch you not gon' disrespect me!"
"I'm tired of you mistreating me."
One thing led to another. Chrissy hit me in my face with her fist. I tried to defend myself, but I didn't want to fight her. She put me in a headlock and rammed my head into the brick wall. She then threw me to the ground.
"You stupid b*tch. Get your sh*t and get the f*ck out my house!"
She grabbed what clothing items I did have and put me out. I had nowhere to go. I walked over to Karen's house and asked her if I could stay there for a while. Karen's mother agreed so I stayed with them for about two weeks.
"What happened Kelley?"
"Chrissy beat me up."
"Why is she always treating you like sh*t?"
"I don't know. She said it's because I had sex with Nippy."
"You had sex with Nippy?"
"Yeah."
"Why?"
"I don't know."
"But wait a minute, ain't that Daminea's boyfriend."
"I guess."
"Well stop crying. You can stay here in my brother's room until he comes home from the service. That's what Mama said. You wanna smoke some weed?"
"Yeah."
Karen and I smoked marijuana and laughed all night. It was nice to be away from the violence and around someone that cared about me. In the morning, I walked to Chrissy's house.
"Chrissy can I come back home?"
"Hell naw b*tch. Get the f*ck away from my window."
"I don't have anywhere to go."
"I don't give a f*ck. I can't stand that b*tch."

Chrissy slammed the window and that was it. I was homeless. I walked back to Karen's house and asked if I could live with them and Karen's mother said her son was home and that there was no room. I walked back to Chrissy's house and stood outside the door. I was sleepy. It was late and I just wanted to lie down.
"Why are you out here?"
"Chrissy said I can't live with her no more."
I don't know why Nippy was there.
"I told you they didn't love you and I was the only one that loved you. You can live with me."

I had one suitcase full of clothes and left with Nippy. My new place of residence was eleven seventeen east eighty first street. When we arrived at Nippy's aunt's house he told me to be quiet and go in the bedroom. His bedroom had a full size bed and a dresser with a mirror. A TV that sat on crates and there was a hole in the floor filled with screen like wire. I guess that's how the water bugs got in. We lived with his Aunt in a two bedroom apartment on the third floor that had a dining room, living room and kitchen. The dining room had a wooden dinette set and an entertainment center that held a television and radio. The entire apartment floor was covered with tan carpet except the bathroom and kitchen. The bathroom was typical and her medicine cabinet was filled with several bottles of medicine.

"Who you got in that room?"
Antoinette had to be in her fifties or sixties. She was fair-skinned with uncombed gray hair and overweight. She didn't have many teeth and wore glasses. Her butt was so huge that it stuck out the back of the chair whenever she sat down. She always wore this beige, silk nightgown basically all day unless she went to church or a doctor's appointment. Antoinette was nice until you pissed her off and she would snap. She was giving and really wanted me to be okay. She was a fun old lady, but was also fickle sometimes. She would help me with bus fare and feed me sometimes, but other times would just flat out tell me no.

"Just a friend and she gon' be staying with me for a while."
"Well who is?"
Nippy never responded
"It better not be no young girls in my house. You gon' get enough of messing with young girls."
"Don't come out the room unless you gotta clean yourself or use the bathroom."
"Why I gotta stay in here?"
"My Aunt just don't want nobody in her house."
"Well why she say you gon' get enough of messing with young girls?"
"Don't worry about her. Just don't let her see you."
"You wanna smoke some weed?"
"Yeah."
I inhaled, choked and coughed so hard I spit up. My head began to hurt and my mouth was dry. Nippy brought me some orange juice in the room. I didn't wake up until the next morning. When I did awake my panties were wet. *How did I never feel anything? I smoked marijuana numerous times and was always somewhat coherent.* I thought. On many occasions I didn't remember Nippy having sex with me. The only evidence I had was his cum oozing out of me. I smoked marijuana, but it didn't make me sleep like I was lifeless. I didn't understand why I didn't wake up. I remembered him giving me orange juice or milk before I went to sleep.

****

"Suck it."
"Suck what?"
"My d*ck."
Nippy smiled.
"I ain't never did that and I don't know how and I don't wanna do it."
I frowned. Daminea told me to suck Jes's penis, but I just licked it. I didn't understand the concept of sucking a penis.
"I did you."
"So. I don't know how and I don't want to."
"Don't you love me?"

"I don't know. I guess. Yeah."
"Well, do it."
"Okay."
"I'll talk you through it."
"Put your mouth on it and just move up and down. Don't let your teeth rub against my d*ck."
"Okay."
"This is nasty."
"Just do it."
"Just go up and down; slow just like that."
"It tastes nasty."
"But you make me feel good. Don't you wanna make me feel good? I made you feel good. Watch your teeth. Come up here and get on top of me."
I crawled on top of Nippy and just sat there. I wasn't sure what to do.
"Sit on it."
"It hurts."
"You'll get used to it. Keep going."
I was no longer motionless with a blank stare on my face. Nippy taught me how to participate in adult sexual acts with him. We smoked more marijuana until I fell asleep.

After school, I made it home and Nippy was sitting on the bed with a joint in his hand.
"Here smoke this."
"I have homework."
"Well, you can do it afterwards."
"Are you hungry?"
"Yeah."
Nippy made some cheeseburgers and french fries.
"You want some juice?"
"Yeah. I'm thirsty."
"Here you go."
I drank some juice and fell asleep. When I awoke it was the next day. Nippy was gone. I hadn't done any homework, my panties were wet again and it was time for school. I jumped up, brushed my teeth, washed my face, got dressed and ran out the door and all the way to Woodlawn and caught the bus.

I went to see my family after school. Chrissy wasn't happy to see me. She always frowned when I came around. I guess it was okay to visit, but not live with her. I hadn't seen Mama in a while, but Daddy did stop by Chrissy's house.
"What you doing over there with Nippy?"
"Chrissy don't want me to live here."
"I sure in the hell don't. Take her with you. She ain't my daughter."
Daddy didn't say much, but he did show me where he lived. I went over his house and ate. Daddy lived in a senior's building down the street from Chrissy.
"You talk to yo' Mama?"
"Naw. She came over Chrissy house one time and spent a night and I stayed there with her. But, after that day she left. Whenever Mama was there Chrissy wouldn't put me out. But, after she left Chrissy told me to get out."
"How are you doing in school?"
"I'm doing okay. I'm getting B's and C's so far."
"That's good. Well, I'll take you back over there. I got some runs to make."
"Can I come over again?"
"Yeah. Just call and make sure I'm home."
"Okay."
"I love you Daddy."
"I love you too Kelley."

The summer was filled with more physical, verbal and emotional abuse. Mama was still absent and Daddy barely came around. The only place I learned to be happy was school. No one knew I was depressed, so I could pretend life was ok without anyone knowing the truth.

I was sixteen years old and a sophomore in school. I gained about twenty five pounds since I started. My weight was up to about one hundred and fifty eight pounds. I wore a size thirteen. I stared in the mirror and cried. I was so depressed that food became a comfort to me. My grades were awful for the second and third term. But, I always managed to bring them up for the second and fourth term. I smoked marijuana every day after school. I needed it like I needed Calgon. It took me to another world where there was no pain. It made me sleep away each day that devoured my soul. Happiness was not within my reach; only death. Many times I went into Antoinette's medicine cabinet and opened her medicine bottles. I thought about swallowing a handful of pills and locking myself in the bathroom so no one could save me.

During my sophomore year, I took a class called Career Prep and was taught how to conduct myself at job interviews. I met with mentors every Tuesday and participated in mock interviews. By the third quarter of my sophomore year, I went on my first interview at Reggios Pizza and got the job. I made three dollars and twenty five cents an hour and worked part-time. I was required to maintain a 'C' average in school in order to keep the job. Josh and Ronald were my supervisors. Josh was about six feet, medium, nice muscular build, dark skinned with a pretty smile. Ronald was the total opposite. He was light skinned, overweight, and not as tall as Josh. I shared my news with Nippy and he told me I had to give his Aunt seventy five dollars a month or I couldn't live there. I didn't have anywhere else to go so I agreed. The summer arrived and I was out of school.

I made more money in the summer so I purchased clothing for myself and other nice items. I bought my first leather trench coat. I couldn't afford to visit the salon bi-weekly so I learned how to perm my hair. I looked real good on the outside, but was dying on the inside. My mask was so thick there was no way you could see the truth. There was no way anyone could see the embarrassment, guilt, shame, worthlessness, pain and anger. I hid it all with a smile, laughter, nice clothes, jewelry and doing a good job at work. Everybody thought I was happy, sexy, pretty, smart and self-centered. If I was, it was all invisible to me. The more I worked around my co-workers the better I became at masking my pain.

I wanted Mama, Daddy or Chrissy to bail me out of that prison I lived in. I wanted my family to love me. I wanted my family to stop getting high. I wanted Chrissy to stop beating and verbally abusing me. I wanted Daminea to stop verbally abusing me. I wanted them to love me. They were my family and I loved them, but the love was never reciprocated.

****

"Be quiet when you go in. My Aunt is sleep."
I walked to the bedroom and Nippy offered me marijuana and I refused. I fell asleep and he tried to stick his di** in me and I stopped him. I didn't want him touching me and wanted out of that house.
"Good morning Antoinette."
"You still got that girl in my house. Ain't she some kin to Daminea?"
"Naw she ain't."
"Well I know she's too young for you to mess with."
Nippy didn't respond to her last comment.

"Kelley I'll let you meet my Aunt, but don't say your real name."
I walked in the living room and I introduced myself as Martha. Antoinette looked and frowned. I didn't understand why he said my name was Martha. Nippy left and I went back into the bedroom.
"Are you hungry?"
"Yeah."
"Well you ain't gotta stay locked up in that room. I cooked so come and eat."
I came out of the room and Antoinette told me to have a seat. She made me a plate of beans and rice and we ate and talked.
"I know you some kin to Daminea and I don't know what's going on, but you ain't got no business here."
"My cousin put me out and I ain't got nowhere to go. My mother left and told me I couldn't live with her and her boyfriend and my father said he couldn't take care of me no more."
"Well Nippy wrong for having you here. You too young and he knows it. You know how to play gin rummy?"
"What's that?"
"It's a card game. I'll teach you."
Antoinette taught me how to play gin rummy and we played until night fell and I went to sleep. After school I visited my family. I got off the bus and saw Chrissy and Chuck walking toward me.
"Hey Chrissy and Chuck."
"Hey Kelley. How you doing?"
"I'm okay."
"You look like a f*cking slut."
"No, she don't. You always got something bad to say about her. You act like you jealous."
"Jealous of what?"
"You look nice Kelley."
"Thank you."

Chuck was Chrissy's boyfriend and he was a nice guy. He didn't beat Chrissy like Kenneth did. He was calm and humble. We walked back to the building and took the elevator to the fifth floor. The elevator smelled like urine. The apartment was a complete mess. There were piles of trash in the middle of the floor and dishes piled high in the sink. There was no food in the refrigerator so I took my last forty dollars and bought food for them.
"Bi*ch I don't care what the f*ck you buy. You can't live here."
"I didn't ask to live here I just bought some food for the kids."
"Well good. Cus yo' ass can't live with me."
After I bought them some food, we played cards and I had some fun. It was getting late and I knew I couldn't stay so I decided to leave.

Back at Nippy's place things were quite peaceful. Antoinette and I were talking more and she told me things I didn't quite understand. So I just listened.
"Baby I don't know where your mother is, but this ain't right. Nippy always messing with these girls that's too young for him and I don' told him he gon' go to jail if he don't stop. Didn't he already go to court for you?"
"Yeah."
"He didn't have no business messing with Damenia. She was too young. How old are you baby?"
"I'm seventeen. My birthday just passed."
"You weren't seventeen when you came here. How old were you when Nippy started messing with you?"
"Nine."
We heard keys at the door and that was the end of our conversation. Nippy was home. We didn't speak another word. I continued to play cards with his Aunt until one o'clock in the morning. I awoke the next day and went to work.

Angie Cowan was my friend at work and a lot older than me, maybe about seven years. She was about five feet seven, light-skinned, slim build with long hair and long fingernails. She was like the family I never had and later on she came to my rescue. Angie fed me on numerous occasions or shared her food with me. She was truly a big sister to me. I talked and cried to Angie in considerable amounts. I met her family and boyfriend and they were very welcoming. I spent a lot of time with her and her family. I wanted what Angie had in a family. Her parents were still together and all her sisters and brothers were very nice to one another. "Angie I'm so tired of my family getting high."
"Well Kelley you gon' have to stop worrying about them and just take care of yourself."
"I went over there and bought some food for the kids and Chrissy didn't give a sh*t. She just told me that I still couldn't live there." "That's messed up and you said this is your cousin."
Angie frowned.
"Yeah. Chrissy."
"Where yo' Mama?"
"She left when I was thirteen."
"Damn. You messed up all the way around."
"Well, don't give up. You'll be okay. As far as Chrissy is concerned, I don't care what's going on. She's supposed to be a role model and that man ain't got no business messing with you."
Our shift ended and Angie dropped me off at Nippy's place. I got there and went straight to bed. I really didn't want to be in that house anymore. I wanted to be with my family. I hated that they used drugs, but I would have done anything to be with them. I awoke for school and had no idea Mama would have to come to my rescue.

"Kelley, are you okay?"
Ms. Rogers was concerned.
I shook my head to the left and right.

"Can one of you fellows take Kelley down to the nurse?" The school nurse called the paramedics and then my mother. The pain worsened while I waited for Mama and Bert.
"You gon' be okay baby. You gon' be okay."
I cried and couldn't straighten my body. I was completely bent over. I had to drink some barium and have an X-ray done. I was given pain medicine while we waited for the results.
"Ms. Porter your daughter has an ulcer and her diet is going to have to change. No spicy foods, no hot foods, nothing with citric acid, no pop and so on. I have a list you can take home with you."

The pain subsided and I begged Mama to take me with her. I cried. I was angry and hurt. Bert didn't want me living with them. I hated the ground he walked on. I wanted to knock him on his head from the back seat. Mama eventually took me back to Nippy's house.
She could've dropped me off at a shelter. How could she bring me back here? I am her daughter. Why doesn't she want me? What did I do wrong? I thought.

I was so hurt. I cried for days. I felt like Mama didn't love or want me. I became angrier as the days passed and I didn't care anymore. Nippy was trying to stop me from going to school and I hated him. School was my outlet.
"If you try to leave the house, I'll beat your ass."
"Go ahead and try to leave. I will shoot your ass in the foot and then where you going?"

I took another step and Nippy pulled out a gun and aimed it at my foot. He pulled the trigger and the noise was just as I remembered. I was very scared. Antoinette came to the room to see what was going on and Nippy just walked out the door. I never said anything. I sat on the bed and cried. I wanted to leave and had no way. I wanted out, but had no one to run to. I fell asleep. Nippy didn't come home and I was glad I didn't have to feel his grimy hands all over my body. I surely didn't want that nasty nut running out of me. It grossed me out. I realized he had taken my bus card and I wasn't able to attend school. I was livid. I didn't have any money. I began to hate Nippy. I hated Mama, Chrissy, Daddy and all my family for leaving me out here to be treated like garbage. I wanted out of that house. Ms. Murphy had already warned me about my attendance. I didn't want to get kicked out of school.

The next day I awoke for school and Nippy was gone again. Only this time he didn't take my bus card. I made it to school and thereafter I went to visit my cousins. Nicki was with Veto. David was drunk. Chrissy was smoking crack and Daminea was nodded out as usual. I was so disappointed when I got there. No one was in their right mind or interested in seeing me. I left and went back to Nippy's place.
"Why the f*ck did you cut up my clothes?"
"You don't need to be wearing that shit."
"You didn't f*cking buy them you bastard!"
Nippy stood there with this dumb look on his face.
"You better shut up."
"F*ck you."

Nippy pushed me onto the bed and walked toward the door and I jumped up and pushed him. He walked out of the door and I cried. I was eighteen years old and a senior in high school. I missed so many days from school because Nippy continuously locked me in that room or stole my bus card. Chrissy never changed her mind. Mama didn't come to rescue me and neither did Daddy. Throughout my entire time there, Nicki was the only one I spoke to on a regular. We stayed in contact via telephone and she always tried to comfort me. I was happy this was my last year in school. I had no idea what I would I do afterwards, but I knew I had to graduate. As soon as I walked in my homeroom, Ms. Murphy wanted to speak with me.
"Kelley you need to go down to the office and speak with the principal."
"Okay."
I walked downstairs to the office and the information I was given was heart wrenching.
"Hi Kelley."
Dr. Berry was the principal at Hyde Park. He was nice, but stern and followed the rules when it came to school policy.
"Hi."
I sat with my arms folded.
"You have missed too many days from school and this is your last warning."
Dr. Berry handed me the pink warning slip.
I skimmed over the information printed on the sheet and instantly started crying.
"Kelley you cannot miss any more days from school or we will be forced to kick you out."
"Is that it?"
I cried.
"Yes you may go back to class."
I exited his office, wiped my face and walked back to class.
This was my last year and I would be damn if I let that Son-of-a-bit** be the reason I don't graduate. I thought.

I went to Nippy's place and pretended everything was okay. I broke the lock on the door so that he couldn't lock me in anymore and every night I slept with my bus card. I didn't smoke anymore marijuana with him and I studied and focused as hard as I could. I was doing great with my attendance and the first term arrived and I received all B's. Thanksgiving was around the corner and every holiday I called Grandma to wish her a happy holiday. This Thanksgiving call changed my life.
"Hey Grandma. I just called to say Happy Thanksgiving."
"Hey baby, Happy Thanksgiving to you too. Your mother is here."
"She is. Can I talk to her?"
"Hold on baby."
"Hello."
"Hey Mama. I miss you and I really wanna come home. Will you ask Bert again if I can live with y'all?
"Hey baby. I miss you too, and I left Bert."
"Are you living with Grandma now?"
"Yeah."
"Can I come live with y'all?"
"Let me ask Daddy."
I paced the floor while I smoked a cigarette and hoped I wouldn't be rejected again.
"Baby girl."
"I'm here Mama."
"Your Granddaddy said yeah."
"Okay. I gotta pack up my stuff and I will be there today.
"Thanks Mama. I love you."
Nippy walked in the door just as I hung up the phone.
"I'm going to live with my mother at granddaddy's house."
I packed my clothes.
"You ain't going no damn where and if you try to leave I'll beat your ass."
I didn't respond. I thought of another plan.
"Hello."
"Hey Angie."
"Hey Kelley, what's wrong?"
"I need to get out of this house and Nippy told me if I try to leave, he would beat me up."

"Do you want me to come get you?"
"Please, but not now. He went to the store and he coming right back. If he leaves tonight I'll call you."
"Okay."
Nippy came back and threatened me again and I kept silent. I didn't want to give him reason to pull that gun on me again. I was afraid and finally found a way out. I needed him to trust me and leave the house so Angie could come get me.
"I don't know why you trying to go live with yo' Mama. They don't want your ass. If they did, you would've never been living here with me. So you might as well unpack your sh*t cause you ain't going nowhere."
"Okay."
"I'm going out and you better be here when I get back."
I unpacked my clothes, slid my briefcase back under the bed and watched TV. I didn't say a word to Nippy. I went into the dining room and talked with Antoinette.
"Antoinette can I use your phone."
"Go ahead."
"Hey Angie, he's getting ready to leave so can you come now. Park down the street and when you see him walk by you can call me and I'll come out." I whispered.
"Okay. I'm leaving now."
I burst out the front door and ran down the stairs. I stopped and looked out the door leading to outside. I stepped out and Angle's headlights appeared as she drove near me. I got in the car and we drove away.
"Thank you Angie."
"You welcome Kelley."
"Where does your grandmother live?"
"She lives on seventy fifth and May. Seventy five thirty seven South May."
"Okay."
"It's about time you found your Mama. You didn't have no business living there and I know that's your family, but all of them are wrong. I don't know how you can have anything to do with them. But, I know it's hard. At least you have somewhere to go now. His ass needs to be locked up."

"It's right here Angie."
"Okay. I'll wait here to make sure you get in."
"Okay."
I exited her car, waved and rang the doorbell. I saw Grandma look out the window and she opened the door.

Reunion-6

Winter 1989
"Janie, your baby's here."

I stepped in and cried as I hugged Mama. I didn't want to let her go. I missed her so much. She was gone for five years and it felt like forever.

"Hey Mama, hey Grandma, hey Granddaddy, hey Aunt Pam."
I was ecstatic about being in the midst of the family again. Nippy had no idea where grandma lived and I was free. My new place of residence was seventy five thirty seven South May. Grandma's house had three bedrooms, a dining room, living room, eat-in kitchen, full finished basement and a backyard. I slept in the basement with Mama, my cousin and her daughter. I continued to work at Reggios Pizza and maintained perfect attendance at Hyde Park. Nippy continuously appeared around Hyde Park harassing me and I really wanted him to leave me alone. Somehow he found out where grandma lived and showed up on her doorstep.

"What the hell is this man doing around my house? Didn't he used to mess with Daminea? Janie he ain't got no damn business being around your baby. You didn't have no damn business leaving your baby and she's been living over there with him! I want his ass away from my house or y'all can find somewhere to go."
I never witnessed grandma so upset in all my years. Nippy left, but that didn't stop him from bothering me. A few days later he called. I don't know how he got the number.
The phone rang.
"Hello."
"Hey Kelley."
"My Mama told you to leave me the hell alone."
"I was just trying to let you know you have mail at my house and it's from that credit card company you applied at."
"Are you gonna be at home?"
"Naw."

"Okay. Well, I will come over and get it after school today."
"Hey Antoinette. Nippy said I had some mail and I just came to pick it up."
"Okay. I guess it's in the room."
I opened the door and Nippy was sitting on the bed.
"Where's my mail?" I frowned.
"It's right here."
"Well, give it to me so I can go!"

Nippy grabbed me and threw me on the bed. I punched, kicked and screamed. He was trying to take my gold jewelry. He held me down with my arm twisted behind my back and took my rings off my finger. Then he hit me in my face. I fought as hard as I could. I managed to get up and tried to run out of the room and he grabbed my leather trench coat. I slung my arms back and let it roll off. I opened the door and he came after me. I picked up the telephone and threw it like it was a ball. He ducked and ran out the door with my leather coat and jewelry.

"Who called the police?"
"I did."
"What's the problem?"
"Nippy called me at home today and told me I had some mail from a credit card company and I came over here to get it."
"Who is Nippy?"
"His real name is Tyrone Brown Sr. He's an old friend. I used to live here because my cousin wouldn't let me live with her."
"Okay, where is he now?"
"He ran out the door."
"Can you give me a description of him?"
"He about five feet eleven, medium build, dark-skinned, ugly and he got my leather coat and jewelry."
"Okay, where do you live?"
"I live with my Grandma on seventy fifth and May."
"It's too cold for you to catch the bus without a coat so we'll take you home. You should put some ice on that eye." The officer said.
"Okay, thank you."

"Kelley give me your phone number in case we catch him."
"It's seven, seven, three, five, five, five, seven, five, three, seven."
"Okay, if he comes around, to your job, home or school, call the police. We'll be in touch."
"What happened to your face?"
"When Nippy called today he said I had some mail over there and when I got there he beat me up and took my coat and jewelry.
"Don't ever go over there again and if he calls here call the police."
I cried. Mama called the school and explained the situation to Dr. Berry and he allowed me three days out of school and told me to bring the report to school.
"Hi Dr. Berry. Here is the police report so am I going to be okay with school?"
"Yes. Kelley everything is okay."
"Thank you."
After class dismissed, I saw Nippy hiding behind a tree across the street and I stepped back into the school building.

"Officer Stanley the man that beat me up is outside and the police told me to tell y'all if he comes around me."
Officer Stanley and his partner were on the school campus daily to make sure there weren't any fights. They walked me back out the building and Nippy was gone. They waited at the bus stop with me and made sure I got on the bus.
"Go straight home Kelley."
I made it home safely.
"Hey Grandma, Granddaddy and Mama."
"Hey Baby."
Mama and my grandparents said hi at the same time. We all laughed.
"How was school?"
"Nippy came up there and I went back into the school and had the police come out with me."
"That lousy son-of-a-b*tch. You did right Kelley; run when you see him."

Mama gave me a big hug and it felt so good and warm. I needed that hug from Mama.
The phone rang.
"Hi, this is Officer Davis. May I speak to Kelley Porter?"
"Kelley the telephone is for you. It's a police officer."
"Hello."
"Hi Kelley. This is Officer Davis and I wanted to let you know we caught Tyrone Brown Sr. We have him in custody now. Write this information down for your court date."

A few months later Mama and I found our own apartment and moved. My wish had finally come true. I was back at home with Mama after five long, hard depressing years. Things were not all peaches and cream. I didn't know I resented her so much. I thought after reuniting with Mama all would be well, but I was mistaken. Mama and I moved into our new studio apartment on the second floor. Our apartment had one living room with a bed that folded upward and into a space that hid behind a wooden door. The kitchen was quite large and so was the bathroom. There was a large walk-in closet to the left of the front door that led to the living room. Life was great. I could finally remove the mask that I had worn for so many years.

"Baby, what time do you have to be in school?"
"Nine fifteen. I only have three classes left before graduation."
"Okay, I made breakfast if you want some."
"I do."
Mama and I sat at the kitchen table and ate eggs, grits and bacon. I didn't speak of anything that happened over the five years Mama was absent.
"I get out of school at eleven forty five and I have to go to court and press charges against Nippy today at two thirty. Will you be home Mama?"
"I gotta go by your grandma's house so if you need me that's where I will be."
"Okay, see you later."

After school, I went straight home and did my homework.

Knock, Knock
"Who is it?"
"It's Nippy."
"You're not supposed to be here and I'm calling the police."
"Please don't call the police. I'm not going to hurt you. I just wanna give you your jewelry back."
"How did you even know where I lived? I didn't give you my address. Have you been following me?"
"Kelley open the door so I can give you your jewelry and leave."

I opened the door and Nippy walked in. I was really scared. I wondered how much damage he would do to me. I was scared he would beat me up again.
"How did you know where I lived?
"Damenia told me where you lived."
"Well, I don't want you around me so give me my jewelry and leave."
The clock moved closer to one thirty and I was supposed to leave and be in court at two thirty. Nippy walked closer to me and I was afraid. He grabbed my shirt and began to undress me.
"Don't be scared Kelley I'm not going to hurt you. You know I love you."
He lowered my pants and laid me on the foot of the bed. I wanted him to leave me alone. I was scared he would hit me so I did not resist. He stuck his d*ck in me and I laid there in disgust.
"I cried. Please get off me. Get off me."
"Don't be scared. Don't you still love me?"
"Just get off me and leave!"
Hours later Mama came home and although she was gone for five years, she knew when something was wrong with me.

"What's wrong baby?
"Nothing. I'm just tired."
"Did you go to court?"
"Naw, I didn't feel like it."

"Okay."

Mama walked into the kitchen. I didn't tell her Nippy came over for the fact that I thought she would get mad at me. I just wanted to be free from his clutches. I took a nice hot bath and went to bed. I slept longer than usual. But, Mama's bacon awoke me. It was already ten thirty, but I didn't have to be at work until two p.m.

"Mama Nippy came over here yesterday and that's why I didn't go to court."
"What you mean he came over here. How the hell did he know where we lived?"
"I don't know. But, I didn't tell him. I haven't talked to him since the last day he called me at Grandma's house. He said my cousin gave it to him. I assumed it was Daminea, but he didn't say."
"Did he do something to you? Did he hit you? 'Cus I'll kill that son-of-a-b*tch if I catch him bothering you again."
"No he didn't hit me."
I cried.
"Things are going to be okay baby. I will make sure he doesn't come around again. It's going to be okay Kelley. I'm home now and I'm never leaving. Clean your face and get ready for work."

Mama hugged me and rubbed my back. A month passed and Nippy never came around again. My family was still using drugs and the only one that ever came around was Nicki. They didn't even know I was getting ready to graduate. Although Mama was back, my heart still ached for the reason that I missed and needed my cousins. My mask wasn't as tight as all the other days I worked. I was more eager to talk and indulge in other conversations. I was ready to talk about me, prom, my grades, our apartment and Mama. I had a new life and was free.

Work wasn't so busy, so after Ronald left, Josh came in and we all horsed around. Josh picked me up and carried me over to the sink and pretended as if he was going to drop me in and all I could think about was kissing him. Josh was twenty five years old, married, handsome and sexy. After that day, Josh and I started a secret affair.

Nippy and Daminea taught me everything I knew about sex and this was the first time I wanted to initiate it with an adult man. Nippy and Daminea were always the aggressors, but this time I was overcome by feelings of infatuation and curiosity of being in a sexual relationship with a man. I didn't hesitate to express myself sexually with Josh. He took me out on a date and we booked a room at a hotel. Josh and I undressed and laid on the bed. I began to kiss his body and maneuvered my way below his navel.

It was about three o'clock in the morning when I made it home. Mama sat on the couch. She smoked cigarettes, drank coffee and appeared to be waiting for me.
"Where the hell you been?"
"Out with Josh."
"You don't stay out that damn long without letting me know!"
"You left me and been gone five years you can't tell me what to do.
Don't try to come back and play Mama now!"
"Don't talk to me like that. I'm still your Mama."
Mama picked up a Pringles can full of pennies and threw it at me.
"You can hit me, beat me or do whatever you want. You left me and you can't tell me what to do. I'm eighteen years old and I ain't gotta listen to you!"

Spring 1990
Prom was around the corner and while in Economics class, one of the finest boys in the school approached me and asked me to attend the prom with him. I agreed.

His name was Griffin and he was very popular for whatever reason. I did not know much about him other than he was popular, handsome and all the girls liked him.

My dress was tailor made. It stopped short at my knees and was metallic maroon and blue. My shoes matched the blue in my dress. Mama said I looked so beautiful. I called my cousins and Daddy so they could see me off. Mama and I waited outside, but they never showed up. None of them arrived; neither Nicki nor Daddy. I was hurt Nicki didn't show up since I was there when she went to prom. She didn't have enough decency to come see me. I didn't expect much of Chrissy, Daminea, David or Allen, but Nicki and Daddy were supposed to have been there.

Griffin pulled up in his maroon Grand Am and off we went to the Marriot hotel located in downtown Chicago. Prom was so much fun. It was the most fun I had throughout my entire time in high school. I danced the night away. Griffin disappeared during prom, but I didn't care. I was amongst friends and enjoyed the best party of the year.

"Kelley do you want to get a room?"
"No. You can take me home and go back to Hyde Park and pick up one of those girls."
Griffin drove back to the school and did just what I told him to do. He picked up a fellow graduate. She got in the back seat of the car and Griffin dropped me off at home.

June 19, 1990
Mama gave me a white and black dress. Daddy picked us up and we drove down to Chrissy's place. Everyone was nice to me. I was ecstatic. I received my diploma for graduating from Hyde Park Career Academy on the honor roll.

"Kelley Porter!"
Dr. Berry called my name and I walked across that stage proudly. My family screamed and shouted. That was one of my better days that I will cherish forever.

I continued to work for Reggios Pizza as a cashier. I applied at Chicago State University for Registered Nurse. I lasted about a week in school and withdrew. My confidence level was about as low as an ant. The classes were a lot larger than high school and I lacked all that was needed to get through a four year university. No one in my immediate family ever graduated from college so there wasn't anyone advice to be given. Over the years, I witnessed some successful families. Some of my friend's parents were successful and I wanted the same. I came from nothing, but I knew people who lived better lives. I wasn't quite ready for college, but I was definitely ready for my Driver's license. In my junior year of high school, I failed the Driver's education class since I almost hit an elderly lady crossing the street. I really wanted my license and I practiced driving in Josh and Angie's cars.

Summer 1990
On my 19th birthday, Josh took me to the DMV so that I could take the drivers exam. I passed and held the key to purchase a car.
Mama and I decided to move into a larger apartment. That studio was not only too small, but it was filled with water bugs and mice. A mouse actually bit me while I was sleeping. Nevertheless, we found a three bedroom apartment. My new place of dwelling was located on the South side of Chicago. It was a lot bigger, but came with more roaches and mice. Mama and I were just happy to have some privacy and more space. I was feeling great. I had a new car, a larger apartment and more money.

"Hey y'all."
Josh was off today and it wasn't too busy. I was scheduled to take phone orders. We joked around as usual. I made a comment about one of the female co-workers who was dating Ted. Ted was another cook who stood six feet two inches and weighed about two hundred and fifty pounds. Ted was upset and threw a wet towel in my face. I threw it back and smacked him directly in his eye.

Ted slapped me and I charged him like a raging bull. We wrestled and he tried to throw me to the ground. I punched and kicked as hard as I could. Ted placed me in a headlock and I grasped a knife that was about eighteen inches long and five inches wide and tried to separate his leg from his body. I swung as hard as I could and the knife landed right in the middle of his leg. His grip no longer controlled my neck. I raised the knife and everybody stepped back. I was ready to chop their asses like onions. I was angry like a wild animal. I refused to be pounded by another man. This time I wasn't going down without a fight. The supervisor interrupted the fight and I was sent home. That was my last day working in Reggios Pizza. Three years and I left with a bang.

I applied for General Assistance after getting fired from Reggios Pizza. I received about one hundred and fifty dollars a month. I searched daily for another job. One particular day after Lonita and I were done filling out applications, we stopped at Walgreens for a few items. When we made it back to my place, I was truly surprised. I parked in front of my apartment building and it never occurred to me that this day would arrive.
"Excuse me Kelley."
I turned around and standing right before my eyes was Beth; Josh's wife. She was tall, dark skinned, medium build and face to face with her husband's mistress. I knew who she was since she visited Josh at Reggios Pizza several times.
"Have you seen Josh?"
"No."
She stared at me and turned away to enter her car. Lonita and I walked into my building.
"Why would she ask me if I have seen Josh?"
"I have no idea, but I know you look better than she does."
"She should've been asking was I dating him; not that I would've told her anyway."
"I'll call Josh and tell him his wife came by, but he's at work and they still don't know we are dating so you have to ask for him." "Okay."
"Reggios Pizza how may I help you?"

"May I speak to Josh?"
"Hold on a second."
"Hello."
"Hey, Josh. Your wife came by my house a few minutes ago."
"Let me call you back."
Josh didn't call back. It was Friday and this was his weekend off so I couldn't call him back. The weekend passed and Josh finally came by.
"I left your Discover card bill under the sunvisor and that's how she figured out we were dating and got your address. I'm not going to be able to see you for a while."

My heart was broken. I couldn't sleep or eat. Time passed and no Josh. I knew where he lived so I drove by his house several times hoping I would see him. Eventually, I caught up with Josh and I was livid. It was a late night and we argued for several blocks. Josh wouldn't listen to me. He walked away and ignored me. I was hurt and angry so I picked up a brick and threw it as hard as I can. The brick slammed right in the middle of his back. Josh continued to walk away from me and I went home.

I continued my job search and after two months of completing applications, I found one at Dove International, the Ice Cream factory, located in Burr Ridge, Illinois. General Assistance ceased and I was back to work. I hoped Josh would call me and every time the phone rang I prayed it was him. A month went by before I talked to him again and when I finally did, it was a big surprise.

The phone rang.
"Hello."
"May I speak to Kelley?"
"Speaking."
"Kelley this is Beth and I want to ask you a couple of questions."
"Go ahead."

"You knew Josh and I were married so why would you have an affair with him?"
"It takes two and you ain't got no business calling my phone and I don't have to talk to you."
"Well he has some habits and are you sure you can deal with them?"
"What habits?"
"You don't know?"
"If I did I wouldn't be asking."
"Well I guess you're going to find out."
I hung the phone up.
What does she mean? Josh has habits. I thought. I wasn't sure how to take that phone call so I just went on with my day. Time went on and no Josh until one night while I was asleep, the phone rang.
"Hello."
"Go look in your mailbox."
He hung up and I ran downstairs and inside my mailbox was a card. I opened the door and turned my head to the right then to the left. I looked for Josh, but he was like a ghost in the night. I missed him dearly.

The doorbell rang.
A month had passed and when I looked out the window and it was Josh. He wasn't wearing that same beautiful smile he usually did upon greeting me. We walked upstairs and into my bedroom.
"What's wrong Josh?"
"My wife left and she moved everything out of the apartment."
"You can live here with me."
"I have a box downstairs. I have to bring it up."
Josh and I sat on the floor at the foot of my bed and he wept like a baby. I had never seen a grown man cry. It upset me to see him in so much pain and I cried with him. Josh moved in with us. Mama didn't mind since she liked Josh and he was very kind to her. Josh and I had some good times while we lived together. It didn't last very long. I learned some things about Josh that I was not happy with and I also learned the truth about my life.

The Truth–7

Summer 1991
"Hey Nicki and Chrissy."
"Hey Kelley."
Finally Chrissy said hi without calling me a b*tch or frowning. I thought.
"We signed up for this school downtown called Bryman campus."
I was shocked Chrissy was nice to me.
"They offer Phlebotomy and Medical Assistance."
"Where is it?"
"Seventeen North State."
"I wanna go. What I gotta do?"
"You have to apply and then complete a Financial Aid application."
"I gotta go back tomorrow."
"Well, I'll ride with you."
"Okay. We're taking the train."
I applied at twenty years old and began my journey in health care. It was a one year program that included an internship and certification exam. During the course, I not only became the class coordinator and the teacher's pet, I learned the truth. After the program, I completed my internship in an Internal Medicine office. Subsequent to that, I was hired as a Medical Assistant. I worked there for about three months, but I quit after I found a better paying job at National Health Labs, located in Elmhurst, Illinois. I continued to push through the pain I was in and Damenia never made it any better. While at home, my aunt visited me.
"Hey Aunt Pam."
"What's wrong Kelley?"
"Daminea keeps telling people I slept with her man and Chrissy treats me like sh*t whenever she comes around. They always got something bad to say about me."

"Baby none of that was your fault. They opened the doors for that man to do that to you; your mother, your father, Chrissy and Daminea. You were just a child. That was their fault. Stop crying."

"So if I didn't do anything wrong, why are they saying it was my fault?"

"Their asses are ignorant. Chrissy and Daminea need their asses whipped for treating you like this and Janie should've taken you with her."

I was in total silence. *For eleven years I was blamed, mistreated, and abused for something I was not responsible for. I'm twenty years old and just found out I was molested and held responsible. I walked around feeling guilty, shameful, and worthless and like the scum of the earth.* I thought. The moment Aunt Pam spoke those words all those feelings turned into anger, resentment, hurt and depression. *How could they do me like this? How could Mama and Daddy keep quiet? All those years of torture and telling me I knew what I was doing; day after day, month after month, year after year, how? How could they make me believe it was my fault? Especially Chrissy, b*tch this, whore that, slut this, stupid that. If I owned a gun, I would shoot all of them dead.* I thought.

Thoughts of suicide invaded my mind. My life took a turn for the worse. The rage and pain were more powerful than ever. I cried every day. Not a day went by where I didn't shed tears. Josh came home and I told him what happened and he immediately knew it wasn't my fault. Our relationship became sexless. I could no longer allow him to touch me. Every touch reminded me of what Nippy did to me. I had nightmares, night after night. I was increasingly afraid of Josh leaving me. Whenever we argued, I planted myself in front of the bedroom door in an effort to stop him from leaving. I was afraid he would never return. I was afraid of him abandoning me just like Mama and Daddy did. I decided to call Daddy and talk to him.

"Hello."

"Hey Daddy."

"Daddy Nippy molested me. All that time I had to live over there at his house because Chrissy wouldn't let me live with her, he was molesting me. None of that was my fault. When I told you what he did when I was nine, you blamed me."

"Baby I'm sorry I wasn't there to protect you. I'm sorry that happened to you."

Instantly I felt better. Daddy didn't blame me anymore. He accepted responsibility for abandoning and not protecting me. I forgave Daddy that moment. My relationship with Daddy was mended and I loved him more. His ability to be accountable for his actions and the fact that he apologized lifted some of the pain from my heart.

Daminea moved in with me after I found out what really happened. I took her and my other cousins out numerous times. I felt a need to be with them and I wanted them to accept me. Although I learned the truth, I still didn't understand what molestation was. Chrissy continuously called me a nasty b*tch and criticized me to friends and family. She almost turned Nicki against me. She constantly told Nicki that I thought I was better than them and Nicki started to believe her. I was so desperate to be with my family. I bought Daminea drugs so that I could spend time with her. It didn't matter. She still ruined my reputation by telling all our friends I slept with her boyfriend. We argued all the time and this argument was the straw that broke the camel's back. Daminea called me every name, but my own; b*tch, slut, whore, trifling and nasty ass. I was fed up and told her to get the f*ck out my house.

I felt more depressed each day. I wore a mask every day. But, this time the pain was heavier than before and I was unable to remove those thoughts of being blamed, molested by Nippy and abused by Chrissy and Daminea. My work production decreased.

****

"Good morning Kelley."
"Good morning Paul."
"What site are you working today?"
"Berwyn."
"Okay. I'll be over there to talk with you during lunch."
"Okay."
Paul was my supervisor at Laboratory Corporation of America (National Health Labs) and a very polite young man. He was white, handsome, dark hair with a slim build. I respected him and the same was reciprocated. Paul always had nice things to say to me. He trusted my work and knew I was capable of making the clients happy. I enjoyed working with patients and it made me feel good to make them smile. I felt a sense of gratification knowing that I was making a difference in someone's life. Paul arrived at my site and we sat outside the office.

"Hey Kelley, I bought you a hot dog and fries."
"Thanks, but I'm not hungry."
"You have to eat Kelley. So what's going on? Your work performance isn't what it used to be and you're not the same person."
"You can talk to me Kelley. I want to help."
"I was molested and my family blamed me. My cousin put me out of her apartment and I didn't have anywhere to go. My mother left me when I was thirteen and my father didn't want me to live with him. I had to go live with the man that molested me. He raped me over and over again."
I couldn't hold my tears back. Paul was quiet for a moment. He handed me a tissue and rubbed his head.
"I'm really sorry that happened to you and I want to help you. Our benefits include EAP. That's an Employee Assistance Program. They offer therapy services and I want you to call them. I can give you some time off work if you need. So take this number and call them when you get home. You don't have to pay anything because it's covered in our benefits package."
"Okay."

"I know your lunch is almost over, but we can sit out here a little longer until you're ready to go back in. I will go in and talk to the office supervisor."
"Okay."
"Well I can go back to work now and thank you for your help. I will call EAP when I get home."
"Okay. Kelley if you can't make it to work tomorrow, call me. Enjoy the rest of your day and things will get better."
"Thank you."

****

"Hi this is Kelley Porter and I work for Laboratory Corporation of America and my supervisor told me to call and speak to someone in this office."
"Are you looking for therapy?"
"Yes."
"I have a few questions to ask you and then we can set an appointment with one of our therapists."
I continued the interview with the receptionist and was given an appointment in Hyde Park with a therapist named Dawn. My appointment was scheduled for the following Monday. I decided to take Paul's advice and take some time off work. My mind was full of rage and infected by Nippy's touch. I was overwhelmed with all the abuse Daminea and Chrissy inflicted on me and scarred by Mama and Daddy abandoning me. I was no longer in my mind. The awful truth had taken over. I went to my scheduled appointment with Dawn and the entire time there, I cried like a baby. I cried so much the session had to be stopped and rescheduled.

I didn't go back to see my therapist, but I did talk with her on the phone from time to time. I told Dawn I wanted to end it all during one of our phone sessions. I really wanted to block the pain out and during my time off work, I sold crack cocaine, smoked marijuana and drank practically every day.

"Are you Kelley Porter?"

"No."
"Well I think you are and you fit the description that was called in."
"What description?"
"Do you mind coming back upstairs with me?"
"We received a phone call from your therapist and she said you told her you wanted to die and that you were going to end it."
I was speechless. I didn't know Dawn would tell on me. I called her only ten minutes ago. I didn't know it was her job to inform the authorities if she suspected her patients of suicide.
"You're too pretty to want to hurt yourself. You have a nice place and nice pictures of yourself. You look really happy or is it all just hid behind that smile."
"Those pictures and this place don't mean nothing. You don't know what I'm going through."
"Why would you want to hurt yourself?"
I never responded.
"Well come on. You're coming with us."

I locked my doors and left with the police. They took me to Little Company of Mary Hospital. The nurse drew blood from me and asked several questions. When the nurse left the room I snuck out and tried to leave the hospital. I was stopped at the door by security. The doctor put some restraints on my hands and after my visit was over, I was transferred to the Psychiatric Ward in Tinley Park, Illinois. This place appeared like a prison on the inside; bars and cots. I was there for three days and the entire time I cried. There was another young lady there and she scared the mess out of me. All day and night she screamed and pulled on the bars. I saw a Psychiatrist there every day and he refused to let me go home. I was not allowed to leave that cell. The only time I could leave was if I had to use the bathroom. After three days the Psychiatrist finally released me.

Jesse picked me up. Jesse was my neighbor and he reminded me of a father. He was tall, dark-skinned, medium build and very kind. I made it home and still felt the urge to commit suicide.

Mama was home and I couldn't look her in the face. I hated her. I was also ashamed of hitting her. Days before, we had an argument and after she slapped me, I slapped her back. I felt so bad. Even though I resented Mama, I knew that hit was a reflex. I apologized and she accepted. However, I no longer wanted to live in the same household as she. I lied and told her I was moving so that she could find her own place. I didn't want to be in the same space as her.

I tried to remain close with Nicki, but our relationship was tarnished because of Veto. He interfered for many years and she couldn't see what he was doing. Nicki was so mean and tried to push me away because Veto was stressing her out and he didn't want me around. I knew what he was doing. He was one lousy and a very abusive man and I refused to watch Nicki in turmoil. I wanted to protect her from Veto, but eventually I started to dislike her. She was doing exactly what Mama did; choosing a man over me. I looked up to Nicki. She was all I had left. We were family and none of them reciprocated the relationship. At this time in my life I began to feel as if I was different from them. They were all mentally unstable and so was I, but I always showed love, tough love and support to my family.

Devastated-8

The type of tragedy in my family was filled with abuse, but forthcoming were devastating blows to my life. Throughout the years, I remained in close contact with Daddy. We spent an enormous amount of time together and were truly father and daughter. I loved him so much and he had found a new love. Annie Hunt was the kindest lady I ever met. I had come to care a great deal for her. She was twenty years older than Daddy so that made her ninety. She was petite, brown-skinned, slim with long hair and very coherent. Daddy and Ms. Hunt shared an apartment on twenty second and Michigan and relied solely on each other. Daddy was happy, healthy, and still his old self.

On the contrary, David disappeared and no one heard from him for almost four years. Life was very difficult for him after that one cold Saturday morning. He was very depressed and one of his most disturbing moments was when he ingested bleach while we lived in the projects. He visited Mama and I on Stewart and Green then disappeared without a trace. During those short visits he always seemed so distressed.

Josh's behavior became suspicious and our relationship was deteriorating. I was unsure of any changes he experienced, but I wasn't satisfied with the results. Josh was not as responsible or reliable as before and I wanted him out of my place. He began looking for an apartment, but his removal was unforeseen.

Mama finally found a place of her own and although I didn't want to be in the same room as her, I needed to find it in my heart to forgive her. Her life wasn't the same after her diagnosis with Hepatitis in nineteen eighty nine. I didn't realize how much I needed and loved Mama. My love for her was blocked by all my pain and resentment.

December 1994
My life drastically changed right before my eyes that one day I received a phone call and was told Daddy was found face down in the snow and had been taken to Michael Reese hospital. I drove over to the hospital and Daddy was no longer the father I remembered. He could barely walk. His speech was slurred and I wasn't sure if he recognized me. I was devastated. Daddy had suffered a Stroke. He appeared to be healthy with tons of energy and without notice it was all taken away from him. But, I never left his side. Through Physical Therapy and the mercy that the Lord had on his soul, Daddy recovered about eighty five percent. After he finished rehabilitation, I had no choice but to admit him to a nursing home. But, I never abandoned Daddy. I moved all of his furniture and shared it with the family. I also inherited his Cadillac and a lot of bills. Daddy needed me to take care of one more thing.

"Where is Ms. Hunt?"
"I don't know Daddy."
"Well go find her."
I had no idea where Ms. Hunt was taken, but I set out to complete my assigned mission. I could tell Daddy was sad and really missed Annie. *Where am I to begin*? I thought. After two weeks of searching and dead ends, I finally found her. After Daddy's stroke, Annie had been moved to a nursing home on the West side of Chicago near Washington and Central. After proving my identity and signing paperwork, Annie was transferred to Alden Wentworth nursing home. Once I signed all the paperwork for Alden Wentworth, Ms. Hunt and I walked to Daddy's room and I told her to wait by the door.
"Hey Daddy."
"Did you find Annie?"
"Daddy you ain't going to say hi to me."
I put my hands on my hips.
"I found somebody for you."
I smiled.

Daddy smiled because he knew I was talking about Annie. I walked to the door but before I could walk Ms. Hunt into the room, the administrator interrupted and informed me that female residents were not allowed in the male resident's rooms. Daddy came out and what a wonderful sight it was to see. Daddy and Annie hugged. Daddy's eyes filled with water and so did mine and Annie's. My heart filled with joy when I saw Daddy smile.

May 1995
Right before Mama moved out, I received a phone call from David on Mother's day telling me he needed to see Mama. I wondered what happened to him. Life had just moved on and no one cared about David. Everyone was so busy with their own lives that he became non-existent. David told me he was living at Alden Wentworth Lakeside on the far North side of Chicago. I called my cousins and asked if they wanted to take a ride to see David. I picked everyone up and drove to the North side of Chicago. This was not the person I had grown up with. My heart was broken. I was in healthcare long enough to know that based on what I witnessed something terrible was happening. Something was killing him slowly.

Mama was devastated to witness David in such poor health condition. We all hugged him and cried. David was no longer the person he used to be. He walked very slowly and every step was like a baby step. The majority of his teeth were missing. His skin was dark and patchy and he appeared to be an old man and was only twenty nine years old. On the way home we all assumed that maybe he had contracted the AIDS virus during his drug use. We remembered seeing medication prescribed for HIV in his name, but he never admitted anything. I dropped everyone off at home and Mama and I went back to our place. Mama was so sad. She cried so much that day. We knew David wouldn't be around for much longer. My heart was heavy for Mama and I knew I needed to forgive her.

June 1995
Mama moved into her own place on the East side of Chicago. She met a very nice man, one who wasn't abusive to her and he took care of her. Lionel Smith was the first man I saw Mama date who wasn't mean and abusive to her. I came to respect and love Lionell. I knew Mama would be okay and I didn't have to worry about Lionell mistreating her. He loved Mama and was by her side the entire time throughout her sickness. He and I took great care of her. After so many visits to the hospital, treatments, medical experiments and watching Mama suffer, I realized it was time to let go of my anger and pain. I realized Mama needed me and it was time. I forgave Mama and focused on her health and making sure she received the best care she needed. I took her to every doctor's appointment and stuck by her side. I even filed for FMLA at work so that my job was protected and I could be there when she needed me. After time passed, I no longer thought of what happened years ago. Slowly but surely, Mama and I became closer and closer. So close I became very protective of her. So close there was nothing I wouldn't do for Mama. My heart was no longer bitter and I was at peace with the fact that Mama abandoned me years ago.

Mama, Lionel and I were a team. Their relationship lasted over ten years and finally ended. He was good to Mama and I and I loved him.

August 1995
Josh's behavior became very doubtful to me. He stopped helping me with the bills and was coming home very late from work. One night he never came home and I assumed he was at his wife's house. I went to her house.

"Who is it?"

"Kelley."

There was no response for a few seconds. Then the door opened.

"Why are you at my house?"

"I'm looking for Josh."

"Well he's not here."

"Okay."
I drove back home and was livid. Later on Josh came home and his jacket was torn and he was dirty.
"Where have you been and what happened to your jacket?"
"I got into a fight." "Are you on drugs?" I asked with an attitude.
"No."
Josh was very calm.
"Well can I test your urine?"
"You don't have to do all that."
"Well you're doing something and I am not putting up with it."
Josh never responded. He continued to bathe and I went to bed. I wasn't sure what was happening to him but he was not the same person that moved in four years ago. I wanted to be there for him, but he refused to be honest. A couple of weeks later Josh left the house and never returned. Right after my twenty fourth birthday, and in the middle of August, I received two visitors.
Knock, knock, knock
"Who is it?"
"It's Detective Burkins and Davis."
I opened the door and two tall white men carrying guns dressed in plain clothes exposed their badges to me.
"Are you Kelley Porter?"
"Yes."
"May we come in and ask a few questions?"
"Sure."
I stepped to the side and allowed them in.
"Do you know a Josh Moore?"
"Yeah, that's my boyfriend. Why?"
"Who is Dewitt Porter?"
"That's my father."
"Why?"
"Well we have a gray Cadillac impounded and it's registered in your father's name, but your name is also listed on the title."
"My father had a stroke last winter and he turned everything over to me. What's the problem? Why is my father's car impounded and where is Josh?"
"We arrested Josh due to his involvement in almost twenty four burglaries between December of last year and now."

My jaw felt as though it hit the ground and my eyes were wide as saucers.
"Do you know anything about this?"
"No I don't."
My eyes filled with tears.
"You have a nice place here."
"Thank you."
"Do you mind if we take a look around?"
"Go ahead."
I slumped in my wicker chair.
"Where is my father's car?"
"It's in the Police pound."
"Why?"
"Josh was driving it when we were chasing him and he jumped out and ran on foot and that's when we caught him."
"So how can I get my father's car back?"
"We will give you the information before we leave."
"Where are Josh's belongings?"
"He has a small box in the bedroom, but I don't know what's in it."
"Do you mind getting it for us?"
"It's back there. Y'all can get it."
"I think this is what we are looking for."
The Detective whispered to his partner.
"We're going to take this box with us and we appreciate your cooperation. Here is the information needed to retrieve your father's car. Have a nice day,"
They searched Josh's box and I really didn't know what was in it since I never looked. They found an orange cap gun with black tape wrapped around the handle. I was floored. I had no idea Josh was committing robberies in my father's car or at all for that matter. He did not appear to be that type of man. He never had any trouble with the law. *The nerve of him.* I thought.

I was enraged. I paid two hundred and fifty dollars to get Daddy's car back. Daddy told me he always saw Josh at the Race Track. I didn't believe him. I saw numerous betting receipts in his pocket, but I didn't think he had a gambling problem. Well come to find out he did. I realized then that Beth was speaking of his gambling habit. I didn't see Josh again until he was wearing an orange jumpsuit and handcuffs. He spent two years in jail after I went to court to see him, our relationship ended. I was hurt, but I moved on with my life.

September 1995
I thought I was done with terrible phone calls and scary visits.
"Hello."
"Hi. May I speak with Janie or Kelley Porter?"
"This is Kelley."
"Hi this is Kim from Loretta Hospital and we have your brother David in surgery and we're not sure if he's going to make it. We've given him several units of blood and it doesn't look good."
My heart dropped.
"Hello. Hello."
"I'm here."
"We need you and your family to get over here right away."
"Okay." I began to cry.
I called Mama at her new apartment and told everybody. I was in total denial. *That's the reason David wanted to see all of us on Mother's day. He knew his time had come to an end.* I thought. I arrived at Mama's place and there was no way Daddy and everybody else would fit in my small Cavalier. Chuck went with us so he let everybody else ride with him. We drove the Eisenhower expressway to Loretta hospital and by the time we arrived, David was dead. He was only thirty years-old and died with AIDS. The site wasn't pretty at all. I pulled the sheet back and we searched for evidence of IV drug use, but never found any. The lesions were like nothing I had ever seen before. We all just stared at each other in total silence. David had gone to his final place of rest. (R.I.P. Brother. I love you.)

Desperately Seeking Love -9

I was twenty four years old and completely focused at work. I received some therapy and started researching pedophiles. The last few years taught me about child molestation and abuse. I learned I was not liable for what happened to me. I lacked the understanding of what child molestation was and its effects. I also still lacked a sense of security within myself. I was still confused and suffering. I desired to be loved. I knew Daddy loved me, but it wasn't complete. There was a void in my heart. Negative emotions were all I felt; vacant and shallow, no self-love, worthless, useless, shameful, and betrayed. I was nothing but an empty casing. I still thought sex was a direction connection to love, so I became notoriously promiscuous. While I felt the inner me was nothing, I always knew I looked good and wished I felt as good on the inside as I looked on the outside.

My house was a police station, dicks in and out. Night after night, I hunted for men and used my body and sex as the key to unlock the door of love. I wanted someone to love me. I wanted love desperately. Not one of them loved me, they only wanted sex.

Four people in one day, it was like three meals and a late night snack. I will never forget this one account. I slept with one man in the morning, another in the afternoon, another in the evening and a woman at bedtime. That was the first time I acted on those bisexual feelings in me. I had no idea what I was doing. The entire act lasted about five minutes. Sex after sex, stalking men, phone call after phone call, tear after tear and drunken stupors was my life after abuse. I was addicted to finding love while abusing myself. I had no respect for myself. I was desperately seeking love. I didn't love myself. How could I love anyone else? How could anyone love me?

"Let me put this condom on."
Lamont was a new sex partner.

"What you need that for? I ain't got nothing."
"Sweetheart, you fine and all, but I like to protect myself." Oh okay. Well, that's fine with me."

After that day, I began using condoms or making my sex partners withdraw. I wasn't concerned with getting pregnant since I was using Birth Control pills. No one taught me about condoms and sexually transmitted diseases. I thank God I didn't contract AIDS. More than often I felt like I was on a treadmill, running and running and not going anywhere just getting off wet. All the men I chased and was left with nothing but a wet ass. It didn't matter to me. I was useless. No one could ever love me. I had several one night stands and hoped they would call the next day. Several times I cooked dinner for men and bathed them in hopes that they would love me. It never happened.

I met a very nice young man. His name was Kevan, and he was handsome and home from the military. The first night he was in the sack with me. Surprisingly enough, he came back the next day. We dated until duty called and we never spoke again. That hurt deeply since I thought we had something special. Thereafter, I was a sperm bank without the use of a cup.
"Girl you know I care about you so come on give me some."
"Okay."
Twenty minutes of sweating, moaning and groaning, and that was the last time I saw him. I called him the next day, and the phone number was disconnected. That didn't stop me from searching for love. Day in and day out, there was always a different man in my bed.
My bedroom door closed, and Officer Perry used my body for thirty minutes and packed up and left.
"Will I see you tomorrow?"
"Yeah. I'll call you."
That phone call never occurred.

Some of my partners were married, in a relationship, single or friends of friends. It didn't matter. I was willing to take a woman's husband so that I could be loved. I was willing to take part-time love so that the void would be filled. I needed that love from a man. I yearned for it night after night.
"Hey baby. What are you doing after the party?"
I met a gentleman named James.
"Why do you ask?"
"Don't you wanna come home with me so I can make you feel good?"
"When are you ready to leave?"
"We can leave now."
"Don't cum inside me."
"Okay baby. I got you."
Wham bam thank you ma'am.

****

"Hey. Come on up. You were supposed to be here an hour ago and what happened to us going out?"
"I was running late at work so I figured I would bring the party to your house."
Calvin was another man I met. Thirty minutes later and I was on my back being humped on and trying to please my friend so maybe he will come back. I got on top and made him scream. That was the last time I heard his voice. *What was I doing wrong? What did I need to change? Did I need to wear lingerie? Should I have performed oral sex on them? What was I doing wrong?* I thought.

I had a wonderful time dirty dancing with him at the club. He noticed and purchased drinks for me only all night. I know he wanted me. We finally made it back to my place. I undressed him and licked all over his body. I made him feel so special. He moaned and enjoyed the pleasures I provided.
"Don't cum in me."
"Okay, baby."

We made passionate love, and I knew I had him. The next morning I made breakfast, and we enjoyed sausage, eggs and grits. We shared a wonderful kiss goodbye.
"I'll talk to you later."
"Okay. Did you enjoy yourself?"
"Oh yeah. But, right now I have to get home."
"Call me later."
That phone call never transpired.
Did I do it right? Did my teeth hurt him? What was I doing wrong? I questioned myself.
The phone rang.
"Hey Kelley, what are you doing? Can I come over?"
It wasn't who I was looking for.
"Yeah, that's cool."
Not even five minutes after John's entrance, I was on my back. Not one kiss, just up and down until his body jerked, and semen swam all over my stomach. I laid there waiting on the deception.
"I'll call you later."

I never responded. I just watched his backside stroll out the door.
I'm just useless. No one will ever love me. I don't know any of their last names. What did that matter? I would never get a chance to wear it. I thought. Every weekend, night after night, week after week, month after month, I searched for a man to love me, and make me feel better about myself. All I identified with was sex. I looked at my clock and it was about one a.m. in the morning. *Who could be at my door?* I asked myself. I rose out of bed, and walked to the kitchen and it was Officer Mike. Instantly I was irritated. He had been here several times, spent many nights, and enjoyed my cheese eggs and bacon.
"What? You want some p*ssy? Come in and get some and get the f*ck out."
I frowned.
"What's wrong with you?"
"All that don't even matter so if you want some let's get it over with. That's all you want any damn way."
"No it's not."

I undressed myself and laid on the bed. Thirty minutes ended with a loud gasp and semen all over my back.
"Now get the f*ck out."
I slammed the back door and cried until morning.
How many men have I been with since Josh left? Close to fifty. What am I getting out of this other than a wet butt? I still feel unloved and unwanted. They are just using me. I hate men. I thought. I developed anger after I realized I was being used and abused. I developed vengeance and had a vendetta against men. I wanted to hurt them for all the pain they caused me. I wanted them to feel the wrath of my pain. Love no longer existed in my heart and I was out for revenge. I was my own worst nightmare. Darkness filled my mind, body and soul. I became a man with panties on. My heart was no longer attached between my legs. It was f*ck them and leave them. I wanted to hurt them just as they did me. So many nights there was a different man. Some of them even crossed each other's path. As one left another was coming. I really believed if I gave them my body they would love me. I was wrong. I realized all I was to them was just sex.
The doorbell rang.
"Hey Reggie."
"How are you doing sexy?"
"I'm fine."
"You ready girl."
"Yeah, let's go."
My friend and I went out to dinner and had cocktails later at a club in the city.
"I had a great time tonight. Thank you."
"Can I come upstairs?"
"Sure."
Ten minutes after talking I was on all four. He had his way with me as they all did. The only difference this time was he had to leave at my order.
"Can I spend a night Kelley?"
"No."
"Why not? You don't have to work in the morning so we can sleep in."

"No, we can't and you have to leave."
"Well, I'll call you tomorrow."
"Okay, see you later."
I awoke the next afternoon and had several messages in my voice mailbox. Three partners called wanting to see me and I had plans for them. I became cold hearted and ruthless. I mastered manipulating men into liking me and then I would dump them like they were garbage. Phone call after phone call and no answer, but, this time I wasn't the one calling. Unexpected visits and drive-bys (Not shooting), stalking, if I would like to say, however, this time it wasn't me.

"Hello."
"Hey Kelley, this is Melvin. What are you doing later?"
"I'm chilling tonight. Why, what's up?"
"I wanted to know if we could hang out again."
"I don't think so and I really don't want you calling my number anymore."
"Why? Did I do something?"
"Naw. I just don't want you calling me anymore. You were just a f*ck and I'm done with you."
"Why are you being such a b*tch?"
"Yo' mama."
I hung the phone up. The phone rang.
"Hello."
"Kelley what's wrong with you?"
"Don't call my damn phone no more!"
Melvin called back several times and left nasty messages on my voice mail and I didn't respond to either of them.
The phone rang.
"Stop calling my damn phone!"
"Hello. Who do you think this is?"
"Oh. Hey Eric, I thought you were somebody else."
I laughed.
"Who else is calling you?"
"That is none of your damn business."
"Well, who did you think I was?"
"You know what don't call my f*cking phone anymore. I don't want your ass. You weren't sh*t but a f*ck!"

I continued on this angry and lost path for some time. I thought I was in control and enjoyed hurting my partner's feelings. I dismissed all of them the same way some of my other partners dismissed me. I got a thrill behind that. *Who's going to be the next victim?* I thought.

I went out on a hunt preying on guys that wanted me and I made sure I discharged all the ones that called back. I was tired of being humiliated and left for trash. It was time for me to take charge. It made me feel better about myself. *My doorbell rang.*

"Hey, I'm coming down."

I pulled my head from under the window.

"What's up Kels."

"Hey John. Nothing much."

I was just about to take a shower. Do you wanna hop in with me? I asked as I walked into the bathroom.

"You know I do."

John undressed himself. The shower was nice and hot and the mirrors started to steam. We washed each other's body and he enjoyed my touch. I could feel his nature rise so I decided it was time to get out.

"Where are you going?"

John stood there naked with his arm resting on the shower pole.

"I'm going in the bedroom."

I grabbed a towel from the rack.

"We can't start in here?"

John rinsed the soap off his body.

"Who said we were starting anything."

"Whatever. I'll be in there in a minute."

By the time he made it out the bathroom, I was lying face down on my bed with a bottle of lotion next to my thighs.

"Can I have a massage?

"You haven't wanted a massage in all this time."

"Well, I do now."

"Yeah, okay."

"Well are you going to give me one or not?"

I raised my arms above my head.

"Yeah, I can."
"What are you doing? I never said we were having sex."
I turned over to face him.
"Well, it's not like we've never done it and damn you got me all hard and I can't have any?"
"No you can't."
I dressed myself.
"What? Are you playing some kind of game?"
"No. You're the one came over here and assumed you were getting some. So the first three letters of assume is an *ass* and that's what you just made of yourself."
I walked towards the front door."
"You know what Kelley. You on some bullsh*t."
 John walked out the door.
"Whatever." I smiled and slammed the door.

That felt good. This time he walked out hard as a rock and I'm as dry as the heat in the middle of the summer. I still feel horrible, sleeping with all these men and I just feel like a whore. No one will ever love me. I don't know why I continue to do this. I wish my life was better than this. I know one day things will get better for me. I thought. Many nights I went out and drank so much, I couldn't remember what happened the night before. There were times I drank so much, I had no business behind the wheel of any car. Many nights I cried, I was depressed and hid it all behind my smile, nice clothes, jewelry and make-up. I told myself I was a player and that I was doing what I wanted to. I told myself I didn't want a man. I told myself I didn't have time for a man. I told myself I was too focused on me and a man would just complicate things. But, I knew deep inside I wanted someone to love me. I never knew a man could never make me feel better about me until later in life.

Ms. Sexable the College Student-10

During the summer of 1996, my friend Karen called me and told me she entertained men as an exotic dancer and made great money. She told me about an advertisement in the newspaper. I called the number attached to the advertisement and set up an audition. I wore a red negligee and red stilettos. After about two minutes of dancing I was hired. My first performance was at a Jamaican club filled with about one hundred fifty people.

"Alright fellows get ready for our newest dancer. She's hot, so get your money ready! Ms. Sexable!"
The D.J played my tape. I walked out onto the stage and there were so many men. I wore a white fitted T-shirt, daisy dukes shorts with white stilettos. I was so nervous my knees knocked. But, the men didn't notice. All they noticed was a beautiful body with seductive moves. Loud screams and yells echoed from the crowd. They loved me. Dollars, fives and twenty dollar bills rolled across the stage. I was excited. I enjoyed dancing and making all those men desire me.

Wow, all I'm doing is dancing in hot shorts and a fitted T-shirt with no bra and I'm making all this money. I thought. My knees stopped knocking and I went into another world. I rolled my hips into a backbend and from there a split. The crowd roared. More fives covered the stage. A gentleman climbed onto the stage and tried to grab me. Without notice, security grabbed him and tossed him right out of the club. I continued on and made a total of two hundred seventy five dollars for twenty minutes of dancing. *This is easy.* I thought.

"Great job Kelley."

Albert was my manager and booked all my shows for a fee. He was tall, heavy set, light-skinned and all about business. Albert was somewhat passive, very respectful and would do anything for me. He was like a chameleon; just as professional as he was ghetto. We were very close and enjoyed each other's time. Albert was not just my manager and security; he was also a good friend.

We worked together for about a year, maybe longer, until I decided to dance independently.

"Thank you."

"They loved you and this is your first time dancing?"

"No. I've competed in dance contests at clubs on the North side and won several times."

"Well that was your practice because you are good."

"Okay let's get you paid."

Albert handed me two hundred and fifty dollars and I really didn't appreciate him taking any of my money since I was the one that danced. But, I didn't say anything since he scheduled my first show. I obtained my stage name from my friend Vince. He and I went to high school together and he was an aspiring singer. After moving to California, Vince visited friends in Chicago and I bumped into him at a local club and he sang one of his songs to me. As I listened, I heard the name Sexable and Daminea and I decided I would use that name as my stage name. I never asked Vince if it would be okay. I figured he wouldn't mind since he did sing the song to me.

During my time as a dancer, I still desired to be loved. Sure I danced in sexy, provocative outfits, but there was no sex, oral sex, penetration or love. I realized I was merely a sex object to all the men that watched my shows or hired me for private shows. I felt I needed the attention. I thought it made me feel better about whom I was. In some ways it did make me feel special and wanted. I danced and people loved me. They weren't familiar with what was really going on with me. All they saw was a beautiful woman with seductive moves and great entertainment. I felt like I was finally being scrutinized opposite of what Chrissy, Daminea, Nippy, Mama and Daddy made me see myself as. In a strange kind of way, I began to feel some love for myself. I realized that I could keep my goodies to myself. I also realized that I was more than just intercourse. I developed a sense of security and arrogance. My confidence was born. I knew if I won contests and performed for hundreds of people, I had to be special in some kind of way. I went from feeling invaluable to very arrogant.

The love I was looking for from Daddy, Mama and my family came in abundance from strangers from the East coast to the West coast. I'm not insinuating that one who feels worthless and searching for love should become an exotic dancer. I am only saying this is the path that I chose to take and fortunate for me, my self-esteem improved a little bit. I experienced a lot of dangers associated with stripping and as you read, I will share a few with you.

Albert scheduled three shows for me this night and I was ready. The only difference this time was they were all private shows and I had to get totally nude. Two were bachelor parties and one was a birthday party located at the Essex Inn downtown. I expected to receive one hundred and fifty dollars per show plus tips. This was worse than my first show at the Jamaican club. I wanted to take the edge off, but I was afraid to have a cocktail. I was afraid I would fall and embarrass myself. So I left well enough alone. I really didn't want the men to stare directly in my eyes so I took my matching shades with me.

Packed in my bag was a red, patent leather mini skirt suit with the red thong, bra and thigh high boots to match. My second outfit was a white fitted mini-dress with back and side openings, white thong and bra with silver rhinestones on the front and white stilettos. The final outfit was some blue jean daisy duke shorts, a white lace teddy and a white patent leather trench coat.
"Damn, she fine."
"Her body is nice. Look at her legs."

"Man, I want to see that body when those clothes come off."
"Sure would love to take her home."
"She got some pretty ass skin."
Sitting in a chair in the center of the floor was the bachelor. I walked beside him and rubbed my body against him. He was thirsty for my attention. I played with the crowd for a while. Lap dances after lap dance. So many tips flooded the floor. My security collected my money and he packed a nine millimeter. I felt comfortable and slowly removed my jacket to expose the beautiful skin that one gentleman commented about.
"Take it off. Take it off!"
It's not time. I'm going to tease them and watch their mouths drop as I slowly remove my red vest and expose flat stomach and cleavage. I thought.
"Ooooooh we she fine. Damn look at her stomach. Her skin is all one color!"
"Take it off!"
I moved my hips side to side in a rocking motion and slowly unzipped my red skirt and exposed my tight ass. More money hits the floor. I bent over and shook my ass in a client's face and he stuck twenty dollars in my G-string. I worked the crowd and finally made my way to the bachelor.
"Yeah baby. It's time for some special attention!"
I gave him a very slow lap dance as he rubbed my ass and arms. I used my feet to clutch the legs of the chair and rolled over into a back bend. His hands gently rubbed my stomach and back up to his face I came. I lifted up to a squatting position on his thighs and my breast embraced his face.
"Oh yeah man this woman is good. I've got to get her card. I want her to do my birthday party!"
"Get up baby."
I moved the chair to the side and laid a white shower liner on the carpet for protection from the water. I pulled the bachelor to the middle of the shower liner and slowly undressed him from behind. He was in total compliance. I had total control. I unbuttoned his pants and let them drop to the floor. The crowd rocked. I rubbed his chest and stomach and quickly yanked his underwear off. Screams and laughter filled the room as he covered his small cock.

"Lay down on your stomach."
I removed my bra and thong and more money hit the floor. My naked body exposed to complete strangers and I was safe.
"Damn, she has a bad ass body."
"I sure would love to take that ass home."
"This bit** is fine. Oh my God."
"Don't call me a b*tch."
I looked the culprit directly in his eyes. Whip cream, Hershey's chocolate and cherries created a sundae on the bachelor's butt cheeks. I bent over and let all the lusting men get a good look at my goodies. The bachelor laid there patient and obedient to my commands. I worked the crowd some more and responded to the request of another lap dance. I walked over to the bachelor and positioned to all four and crawled to his butt. There were plenty of dollars, fives and tens awaiting my presence. I slowly stuck my tongue out and licked the whip cream; making sure not to touch his ass. The crowd went crazy. *They must think I licked his ass. I don't think so. I'm not that desperate anymore. This is all business.* I thought.
I smacked the bachelor directly on his ass and he jumped. More, more, more the crowd yelled. I grabbed my bucket of water along with my sponge and Dove shower gel. I lathered the sponge and proceeded to wash my body.

"Oh she is so sexy!"
"Will you marry me?"
I couldn't control my laugh this time. These guys were making comments that blew my mind. I slowly massaged the bachelor's body with mine.
"Turn over."
The bachelor turned over and I handed him the lathered sponge and he proceeded to wash my upper body. He then rinsed my body and covered it in baby oil.
"Lord have mercy."
"My turn!"
One of the audience members thought he was going to get some special time.
I looked up and slowly shook my head from left to right.

"Damn I gotta have a birthday or get married to experience this.
Well hell I'll just have a party."
The music was down to the last five minutes.
"Stand up. Pick me up and hold on tight."
I wrapped my legs around his chest and fell into a backbend and with the use of my strong abdominal muscles, I rolled back up and my breasts met his face. I let my oily body slide down his.

The music died. I took a bow, collected my gatherings and carried on to the bathroom. Shouts, screams and hollers ranged from deep pitched to high pitched voices. So many compliments; I had never heard so many before. I cleansed my body and tidied up their bathroom. I stared in the mirror and smiled. I felt proud. *Finally no intercourse and men actually enjoyed me for my entertainment. I'm important. I'm wanted and needed just for my entertainment.* I thought. My next show was to begin in forty-five minutes. I walked out of the bathroom and claps filled the room. I smiled and walked toward Albert as he gave them his pager number so that he could be reached when I was needed again. I made a total of two hundred and seventy dollars for twenty minutes of dancing; no sex, oral sex or penetration.
"We will be in touch!"

Some of the men wanted me to dance for them at a later date. My next two shows were just as rewarding as the first one. I made a total of five hundred and thirty dollars between the last two shows bringing me to a sum of eight hundred dollars for one hour and fifteen minutes of dancing. I stuck with my four rules, no sex, no oral sex, no penetration (not even a finger) and do not call me a b*tch. If the rules were broken my show was cut and I walked with the money, since I was paid up front and my security was a licensed gun carrier or a police officer.

Throughout my first six months I worked with Albert, I met several other dancers and inquired about how to retrieve my own business cards as well as a tailor so that I can have original outfits made. I received all the information needed. After about a year of dancing for Albert, I became my own manager.

I went to local clubs throughout Chicago that hired dancers and promoted myself. I had several outfits made and my business cards were ready, however, I was oblivious to how much Ms. Sexable would be demanded.

Spring 1997

I re-applied for the Medical Laboratory Technician program at Malcolm X. College and found a new job at The University of Chicago Hospitals. Back in two thousand five I applied at Malcolm X. College, but I quit due to stress. I never forgot daddy telling me to go to college to become an RN, but after working as a mobile Phlebotomist at Lab Corporation of America, I stumbled across this career in health care. Now I was a college student, dancer, and a Patient Care Technician (PCT). My job entailed phlebotomy, administering breathing treatments, starting IV's, chest physiotherapy, performing EKG's and assisting with medical emergencies. My new job as PCT was very fulfilling. Life was extremely busy since I danced on Monday, Wednesday, Thursday, Friday and Saturday night. School was Monday, Wednesday and Friday and I worked as a PCT on Friday, Saturday and Sunday evening.

"Coming to the stage, Ms. Sexable!"

My show was located in a nightclub in the city called What's Popping. This club was known for having dancers and my time had finally arrived. Packed with two hundred people and in less than five minutes the stage would be all mine. The show was for fifteen minutes, no nudity and paid seventy five dollars. I dressed in my seductive army outfit with the thong and bra to match and black boots. My water gun was attached to my back and ready to blast at the appropriate time. Music *Left, go left, left, go left*. I marched onto the stage and stared out into the crowd. There were so many people who waited to see my most popular show. I rocked and rolled to beat of the music. Lights flashed from the audience. *Wow, all this for me.* I thought.

On the expected beat of the song, I removed my water gun and gave it to the tall, dark security guard standing on the stage. I ripped my jacket off to expose my army print bra and belly chain. I walked closer to the edge of the stage and shook my breast in one of the audience member's face. He threw a ten dollar bill on the stage.

"Take it off!"

"Take it off!"

I was in charge. They had to wait until I heard the appropriate lyrics from my music. However, the lyric I expected would not be the one they awaited. I swayed my hips from side to side as I walked toward the security guard.

"Put the gun on my back."

My water gun was positioned and ready to blast the audience. The lyrics played and I sprayed water all over my chest as a distraction.

Music, *Boom, Boom, Boom, Boom.* I pointed the water gun toward the audience and sprayed them. Heads ducked like it was a drive-by shooting on the South side of Chicago. The audience shouted out of excitement. They were surprised, but satisfied. I gave the water gun back to the security guard and faced my back to the crowd. I slowly removed my pants only to expose my new tattoo on my left butt cheek. I exposed my other cheek and as the anticipated lyrics played. I used my muscles in my butt cheeks to dance to the music and raised them one cheek at a time. The crowd was louder than ever.

"That ass is tight." The owner smiled.
"Yes it is and it looks damn good."
My tips grew wings, dollars, fives, and tens soared through the air and onto the stage.
"Give it up for Ms. Sexable!"
Yells ripped through the crowd like lightening through a tree. They were pleased. I took a bow, grabbed my money and exited the stage. I felt real good on the inside. I was popular and loved for my talent, body and looks. As I walked through the crowd more than half of the audience wanted my card, including women. I received so many compliments. My head grew bigger and bigger.
I danced throughout the Chicago area as well as the neighboring suburbs. Oakbrook, Lombard, Aurora, Naperville, Matteson, Richton Park, Justice, Rockford and it didn't stop there, my presence was demanded in other states as well, Indiana, Michigan, Alabama, Wisconsin, Minnesota, Cleveland, Georgia and Texas. My clients ranged from drug dealers to nine to five men and women; Entrepreneurs to Professional Football, Baseball and Basketball players. I was making more money than I had ever seen in my life and was now a traveling dancer on an all-time high.

People knew me everywhere. Some loved me and some hated me. Some respected me and some disrespected me. None of that mattered. I felt good about myself. No one knew where I'd come from and I now had somewhat of an idea of where I was going.

****

I walked through Malcolm X's lunchroom and young men and women stared and made comments. One was even bold enough to throw some crumpled up money at me. That didn't stop me. I held my head high and walked to the grill area and ordered a chicken sandwich. I sat at my usual table with Yogi and Katina. They were my classmates and friends. They benefited several times from the tips I made during my shows. Numerous days I bought them lunch.
"Excuse me young lady."
I looked to my left.
"Will you come here for a second?"
I rose from my chair and walked over to the older gentleman. He stood by the exit sign to the left of the kitchen and was tall, medium brown skinned, some gray hair, wearing a black suit and an I.D. badge.
"Do I know you from somewhere?"
"I'm not sure, maybe here. This is my second term."
"Naw. It's not from here."
The Professor's face was wrapped in suspicion.
"Well I'm not sure."
"Do you hang on the West side? Where do you live? Where do you party?"
I'm sure he knows me from dancing, but I don't see a need to tell him. I thought.
"No I don't hang on the West side. I live on the South side of Chicago and I party downtown and on the North side."
"Ahhhh. I know where I know you from. You're a dancer aren't you?
"Yeah I am."
"You did a show for a friend of mine. His son was getting married.
You did a great job."
"Thank you. I'm going to go and finish my lunch before my next class starts." I turned to walk away.
"Okay. Do you have any cards with you?"
"Yeah I do."
I turned and stared him directly in his eyes.
"Can I have one?"

If I deny this man my card, it's going to spread throughout Chicago like the plague. Then I would appear to be snobby and snobs didn't receive much business. I thought. I opened my purse and gave the professor one of my business cards and it felt a little strange. I was in school and wanted to keep dancing separate, but that was the price I had to pay. It didn't matter where I went; someone was familiar with me and they always wanted a card. I knew in this business if I wanted to make money; refusing to give up my card wasn't an option.
"Here you go. Have a good afternoon."
I walked away.
"Thank you Ms. Sexable."

Summer 1997
I started to feel disgusted with the whole idea of stripping. I felt like I was being molested again. I remember this one client flew in from Michigan once a month for a private dance. All of my attention was directed to him. I hated doing shows as such.

"This dude must be a damn pervert."
I shut Dean's car door.
"Yeah, but he sure does pay."
"Whatever."
I walked into the lobby of the Essex Inn downtown.
Mitch had already booked his room and was waiting for me. Surely I was impressed, but disgusted simultaneously. Up to the fifteenth floor and the elevator door opened.
Knock, knock.
"Who is it?"
"Sexable."
I frowned.
"Hey baby. How are you doing?"
Mitch had this huge smile on his face.

"Hold on Sexable. Let me inspect the room before you come in." Dean placed his hand on his pistol. That was routine for my security. Whenever I had to perform for this particular client, my security thought it was a little weird so he always paid extra attention. We wanted to make sure he was alone since that was the agreement.
"Okay Sexable. Everything is okay."
Dean held the door open for me.
I walked in and straight to the bathroom. I was familiar with this hotel and there was no need to tell Mitchell, my client, how to arrange the furniture since this was his fourth time requesting a private dance. My security stood outside the door as I dressed.
"Dean, will you play this tape in five minutes?"

Dean was about six feet four inches, two hundred and sixty five pounds and packed a loaded gun. He grew up in the Englewood area and was very callous. He would snatch a Bee right out of the air and kill him with his hand. His voice was very deep and his presence intimidated people. However, he was very protective of me.

Music played. Y'all get ready for the hottest dancer in Chi-town and wanted from all around town and sexyyyyyy, Ms. Sexable!
I walked out the bathroom wearing a red hooded sheer cape, red stilettos, red banded outfit with matching thong and bra with matching finger and toe nails. I turned and allowed the cape to rise just above my hamstrings so he can gain a peep. I could tell he was lusting already. *Freak.* I thought.

He sat there in the middle of the room in a brown chair waiting to lay his grimy hands on my body. I slowly walked around the chair and his eyes followed mine. I stopped in back of him and rubbed my breast against his head. I straddled his lap and performed a very slow lap dance. All twenty eight of his teeth exposed. I slowly removed my cape and exposed my banded body. That was just what he waited for. He grabbed my ass and I wanted to smack him. Thoughts of being molested invaded my mind and I wanted to get the hell out of there. Ten minutes passed and now it was time for me to strip and begin my center show. I erased those thoughts and remained focused on giving a satisfying show.
"Get up baby."

As he rose from the chair I used my body to gently push him on the couch. I moved the chair over by the window and laid my shower liner on the carpet. I beckoned him with one finger and he quickly walked my way.
"Stand here."

I removed his jacket and unbuttoned his blue button down shirt to expose his six pack and Rolex watch. Grabbing his bulging biceps, I turned his back to me and unbuckled his belt. He wore blue Calvin Klein underwear and smelled delicious. *Damn he smells and looks good. His body is such a turn on. Oh well. I can't mix business with pleasure.* I thought. I lowered his pants as he lifted each foot so that he could remove and lay them on the couch. *His suit must have cost five hundred dollars. It's definitely a designer. He never lets me remove his underwear and that is all right with me. I don't want to see that little pecker anyway.* I thought. I rolled my hips and laid on the shower liner. I grabbed my ankles and rolled my thighs, hips and stomach toward the ceiling. Mitch licked his lips and stared at me. I turned over to lie on my stomach and positioned on all four. I grinded the shower liner in hopes of sending his imagination through the roof. I stood up and into a backbend I went, and flipped over into a split.
"WOW."

Mitch was excited and threw money on the floor.
I crawled toward him and through his legs. He slapped me on my ass.
"Not so damn hard!"
I turned and glared into his eyes.
"I'm sorry baby."
I stood to my feet.
"Lay down."

I poured soapy water onto his chest and slid my body all over his. I dried his body and let him dry mine. He poured body oil all over my breast and I rubbed my breast onto his chest. The song next to the last played and three minutes were left. I laid him on the liner, stood over him and removed my thong right in his face. He stared right at my crotch. I swayed my hips from left to right and poured baby oil down my back as it dripped onto his face. Mitch smiled with satisfaction; *job well done.* I thought.
Music. Give it up for Ms. Sexable.

I took a bow, grabbed my belongings and walked into the bathroom. I made two hundred and sixty five dollars for twenty minutes. *Not bad.* I thought. I had two more shows this night so I quickly rinsed his hand prints off me, dressed, thanked him and said goodbye. We drove to the lower South West side to a private party.

"I'm glad that's over. He gives me the creeps."
"I hear you Sexable, but it wasn't that bad."
"Hell you weren't dancing for his weird ass. I was."
"You got one more show after this one right?"
"Yeah, why?"
"I'm tired."
"From what, you ain't did nothing."
We laughed. We exited the car and there were three Hispanic gentlemen waiting on the porch. They were all dressed in suits and looking good.
"Are you Sexable?"
"Yes I am." I licked my lips.

"Damn you fine. Come on in."
We entered the house and it was beautiful and so were the men. Black, Hispanic and White, but those weren't the colors I was interested in. I was concerned about one color; green and how much this mix of men was going to share with me. I enjoyed dancing for fine men. It was great being able to control them with a twist of my hips and a shake of my ass. Lord knows fine men always tempted me.
"Where's your bathroom?"
"Up the stairs and first door to the right and how much do I owe you?"
"My shows are one hundred and seventy five dollars."
"Okay that's cool."
"Here's your money and do you have your own music?"
"Yeah. Here's my tape and my security Dean will tell you when to play it."
Music played. *Ain't nothing but a gangster party.*
I strolled downstairs in my black and white pinstriped mini skirt suit with the hat, cane, thong and bra to match.
"Yeah baby."
"Bring it on. Damn, she got some nice legs!"
I'm about to get paid. These Niggas got some money. I thought as I walked into the living room.
"Bring it over here shorty!"
I popped and rocked my hips to the beat of the music and then I ripped my jacket off and threw it in one of the audience member's faces.

"Yeah baby. Take it off!"
Music; *shake it, shake that shit to the left, shake that shit to the right.* I shook my breast from side to side and then my ass. I couldn't control my laugh. The bachelor had already begun to remove his clothing. *The crowd laughed.* I pulled out my shower liner and laid it on the floor. I maneuvered my way over to the bachelor and grabbed his hand and walked over to the liner. I grinded him from behind and unbuttoned his pants. Without notice, I pulled his pants down to his feet and then his black underwear. The crowd stared at his midsection, but no

laughter. *He must be well-endowed.* I thought.

"Lay down on your stomach."
"Whip cream baby!"
I created his butt cheeks into a cherry sundae and left him there as I worked the crowd. S*ince you want to be naked so bad, there you go.* I thought. *Wow, I'm going to take pleasure in this. There are so many fine men in this room.* I thought. At that moment, thoughts of being molested plagued my mind and I tried to block it out. With no luck, I walked over to the finest man in the room and gave him a lap dance he wouldn't forget. I began to enjoy the lap dance since he was one hot fellow. I was aroused. The thoughts of molestation evaporated like fog in the night. One lap dance after another, splits, backbends, catwalks and seductive moves was the highlight of the bachelor's night. The bachelor was in for a surprise. I crawled back over to him on my knees and rolled my midsection right in his face. He stuck his tongue out. *How gross. Covered in plaque.* I thought.
"Yes, yes, yes, yes!"
"Wooo. I'm loving this!"
"I sure would love to take her home!"
Crawling over his body with my stilettos toward his shoulders, I licked the piled high Whip Cream and ate the cherry. Men screamed and shouted Hispanic language. There was money everywhere.
I smiled, sat up and grinded his back.
"Ooh wee."
SLAP! Whip Cream and chocolate splattered around the room. Standing to my feet, I undressed myself down to my birthday suit. I removed my sponge from the water and lathered his backside and rubbed all over him with my body.
"Are you sure you want to get married man? Cus you look like you in love."
Let me see what the crowd was so scared of. I thought as I grabbed his shoulder. The bachelor turned over and yes he was huge. I lathered my sponge and gave it to him. My breast became the center of attention.
"Dry me off."

I poured baby oil all over my breast and rubbed it onto his body.
Five minutes left. Let me go back to that fine ass man. I thought. I walked over to him and he became my personal masseuse.
"Give it up for Ms. Sexable."
I walked over to the bachelor, whispered congratulations, and took a bow and straight to the bathroom. *Wow. I made six hundred dollars plus some odd dollars for twenty minutes of dancing and nudity.* I thought. My last show was worth about the same and for one night and one hour of stripping, I made fourteen hundred dollars. *Damn I'm good.* I thought.

"Man Sexable you cleared a nice piece of money tonight."
"Tell me about it."
I recounted my money.
"Here is your seventy five dollars and gas money."
I gave him one hundred dollars.
"Thanks Sexable."
Dean shoved his money in his pocket.
"You're welcome."
"I'm just glad that's over. Men are something else. They act like they have never seen a beautiful body."
I lit a cigarette.
"Naw. Sexable your body is not just beautiful. Your face is pretty. You don't do nothing slutty like these other strippers and your moves are damn, smoking hot. You're sexy and you don't take no sh*t from no one. All that's a turn on for a man and these guys already know who the nasty strippers are. You are making easy money girl."
"Yeah well when I finish school, I'm quitting."
I blew smoke rings.
"What you in school for?"
"Medical Laboratory Technician."
I'm supposed to be in school for Nursing. I thought.
"Oh that's good girl."
"I knew it was something else about you."
"Why you say that?"

"Because you don't seem like the type to make a career out of dancing and you smart."
"I don't see how any of these strippers can do it for more than five years."
I dumped the cigarette butt out the window.
"Yeah that's true, but there's a lot that have been dancing for more than five years."
Dean parked the car in front of my building door.
"Well come on. Let me get you upstairs safely. How many shows will you have tomorrow?"
Dean grabbed my bags.
"Four, but I might give one away."
I inserted the key into the keyhole.
"What time is your first one?"
"Seven."
I entered my apartment.
"Okay. I will be here at 6 o'clock tomorrow."
"Okay. Thanks Dean. Drive careful."
I closed my door."

I dropped my bag at the front door. My heart was heavy and my eyes filled with water. I turned the shower on and took a nice hot shower. *I wish I could wash the first layer of skin off my body. Those creeps and their touches disgust me. I want out of this life. I don't like dancing anymore. But, I can't quit now. I only work part-time and full-time isn't available. How would I pay my bills? I'm going to go to work and see if a full time position is coming up soon. I cannot take this. I hate what Nippy did to me. I hate my family for blaming me.* I thought. Thoughts of being molested and abused overwhelmed my mind. I dropped to the floor in the shower and cried.

****

I decided to give one show away since four would have been too much. It was typical of us to give shows to another dancer if we were overbooked. All it took was a phone call and share the information. It was just that simple. I had three private parties; a Professional Baseball player, a Car Dealership owner, and one house party. I decided to take Daminea and Nicki along with me. I drove up to the gates and when they opened, I was floored. I entered what looked like a mansion and I couldn't believe my eyes. I danced for some rich men before, but this was by far the finest house I had ever been in. This house reminded me of the houses on the TV show MTV Cribs.

I'm guaranteed to make some money here. I thought.
Music played. I walked out to the beat of Lil Kim in my black fur coat, black chaps with purple fringes, short matching jacket with thong and bra and black stilettos. My hair was completely blonde and I was ready to seduce. Generally when I performed, the crowd loved me and wasn't afraid to express it. This guy and his friends were extremely quiet and seemed uninterested. I popped my ass and twirled my hip. I did my signature move and no yells or screams. I was pissed off. I thought my center show was guaranteed to get a response, however, no small peckers to expose. *Everyone is too good to participate. I have to improvise.* I thought.

I laid my shower liner in the middle of the floor and slowly undressed myself. I created a cherry sundae right between my breasts.
"Man you better go over there and lick that."

Finally a response. But I don't think so. I thought. The birthday boy walked over and removed some of the whip cream from the center of my breast and sucked it off his finger in a slow seductive manner. I smiled. I ate the cherry and rubbed the whip cream and chocolate on my breast. *These guys are hard to please.*

I guess being as rich as they are, beautiful women come a dime a dozen. I thought. Lathered with soap, I gently washed my breast and stomach. I laid in the middle of their floor. I lifted my ass off the floor and removed my thong exposing my bald crotch. I dried my body and let the oil flow down my back like wax from a candle.

Ten minutes left. Thank God. I thought. The energy produced from the crowd was like Garfield. I finished my show and thanked them.
"Sexable."
I walked towards the exit.
"Yes."
"Can I talk to you for a minute?"
"Sure."
"Can I have one of your business cards?"
"Sure."
"Do you mind if I take you out sometime?"
"I'm sorry I don't mix business with pleasure."

I walked out his door. Mr. Clay was a Professional Baseball player and who knows where I might be had I answered yes to his question. I was actually offended that he and his friends didn't respond the way I expected. So there was no way I was going to give him what he desired. I dropped Nicki and Daminea off at home and continued on to my next shows. The next two shows were successful and between those and the first one I cleared eight hundred dollars. However, the last one definitely warranted the use of Dean's .three fifty seven. Not in the best neighborhood, Dean parked his car and we climbed three flights of stairs and into a killing zone. This was probably one of the most ghetto and dangerous neighborhoods I'd ever danced in. (Englewood)

Knock, knock. The door opens without the screening process.
"We've been waiting for you. Come on in."
The host opened the door.
"Where's your bathroom?"
"Come on. I'll take you."

Dean and I followed this gentleman down the corridor and made a right into the bathroom. It was surprisingly clean.
"That will be one hundred and fifty dollars."
I stuck my hand out.
"We have to pay before the show?"
"Yeah."
"Oh. Well let me go get it."
"They seem ghetto as hell."
"Don't worry about it. I got you."
"Here you go Sexable."
"Here's her music and I will let you know when to play it."

Police sirens. Fellows listen up. Be on the lookout for a lady that's short, built and dressed to kill. She's known to travel with a snake and goes by the name, Ms. Sexable! I walked out with my sheer, white body suit outlined with green rhinestones, green thong and bra, white stilettos and a sheer green hooded cape. *Yells and hollers filled the room.*
"Man ain't gonna be no oral sex, penetration or sex and don't call her a b*tch because she will cut her show!"
That was the first time my rules were announced by a member of any party other than me. I appreciated that. That announcement made me feel comfortable and I thought I would be respected. Plenty of men to lap dance. The birthday boy was very accommodating given that he had no problem exposing his wiener to the room. My center show was the usual and going very well. I was down to my bare ass and at the part where the birthday boy lathers my body. Before I knew it, he quickly shoved his finger up my crotch and I tried to put his eye out with my stiletto.
"You stupid motherf*cker!"
I had flashbacks of being raped by Nippy and went into a rage.
"I saw that sh*t and the show is over."
"What the hell happened?"
"Your lousy ass friend just violated me and my motherf*cking show is cut!"
"You heard her. Shows over."
"Whoa, whoa, whoa. What did he do?"

"He stuck his finger up my p*ssy and this show is over!"
"Sexable go get dressed and I'll stand outside the door."
"Man I told your ass the three rules and now she got my f*cking money and about to leave!"
"Well try to talk to them?"
"You think I'm not. They got my damn money."
"Sexable walk straight to the door. Here are the keys. Go to my car and lock yourself in and if you have to drive off, do it."
"Hey man can I talk to you for a minute?"
That minute I walked out the door and quickly ran downstairs and into the driver's seat. I started the car and was ready to make the first perpetrator a hood ornament. Minutes later Dean came running to the car with his gun in his hand and I jumped over to the passenger seat and we took off.

"What happened up there?"
"Man them motherf*ckers wanted their money back and was trying to stop me from leaving. I pulled out my strap and well, I'm here. So it's all good. Just remember that address and don't ever dance there again."
"You ain't gotta worry about that. I'm not dancing in this damn neighborhood again. I'm glad we got the hell out of there before anything else happened."
"Sexable I wasn't going to let nothing happen to you. If I had to put a bullet in one of those niggas, I wouldn't have had a problem."

The fall approached and most of my shows were at clubs. Every Wednesday I danced at Micasa located in Markham, Illinois. This was a tip show and I always made anywhere from one hundred to two hundred fifty; sometimes more on a great night. A club filled with over one hundred men waiting to feel my body up with their hands. *Another night of hell. The good thing is that I could leave the building whenever I was ready.* I thought. At least ten dancers and we were introduced one at a time. We were allowed a few minutes on the stage then thrown out to the vultures. This particular night I learned about bisexuality and the use of drugs amongst dancers. I really didn't understand the relation between bisexuality, drugs and stripping. I didn't even drink before a show. While we dressed and prepared for our show, several of the other dancers discussed what male and female stripper they would have liked to or had sex with. I sat on the counter top and listened. One of the dancers assumed that I had already been with women sexually.

"So Ms. Sexable who have you slept with?"
Shorty was another dancer and was convinced I had slept with women.
"I haven't slept with any women. I don't get down like that."
"Yeah whatever girl. I would love to lick you up and down."
"Too bad 'cause it ain't going to happen."
"You have been with a woman before."
"The most I've done is sucked a woman's breast.
I glared at Charmaine. Charmaine knew that woman was her. She stopped by my place so that we could car pool to our shows and I sucked her breast. Being funny and aggressive, Shorty decided to put her head between my legs and I pushed her so hard she fell into the bathroom door.
"Don't get your ass whipped."
"Aw Sexable you got a bad ass body and you need to let me take care of you.
"Not."
Yea I have been with a woman and it's none of your business. It only lasted about five minutes. I thought.
"Coming to the stage, Ms. Sexable!"
I wore an orange wig with the matching orange banded suit with the thong and bra to match. The crowd roared. I danced on stage a few minutes and did my signature move; the split.
"Come over here baby."
"Come get this money!"
"Sexable I love you!"
"Okay ladies, y'all got about twenty minutes left!"

I couldn't tolerate another hand on my ass or breast. *My time is up.* I thought. I walked backstage, got dressed, and disappeared. Driving sixty five miles per hour on Northbound on Interstate Fifty Seven, I noticed a car with blue headlights in my rear view mirror. I thought that was kind of cool, but every peep out my rear view window were those blue headlights. I switched lanes and a half mile later, the same blue headlights.

Is this dude following me? If so, I need to be sure. I asked myself.

I switched lanes and a half mile later, I saw those blue headlights. *I'm tired, but I'm not about to go home and allow this pervert to see where I lived.* I thought. I was scared and almost panicked. I switched lanes, one more time. To the far left and lane after lane, there he was.

Should I call the police? Should I exit at one eleventh Street and drive to the police station? I thought. *Okay you asshole. You wanna follow me; well come on. I have a full tank of gas, plenty of money and my cell phone.* I said to myself. I drove right past my exit switching lanes and laughing. Straight to the Congress exit and just then my pursuer dashed to the right and exited the Dan Ryan.

"Now you asshole."

I exited at Congress and re-entered the Dan Ryan and drove home while staring out of my rear view for those blue headlights. That was one scary moment. I never even gave any thought to what could've happened if I hadn't paid attention to those blue headlights.

Six North East was my assigned unit at the University of Chicago Hospital (U of C). I did a wonderful job and was always reminded of why I should become an RN. So many people had more faith in me than I had in myself, doctors, nurses and other fellow Co-workers was assured that I could become a great RN. Anna Mooyen was short, petite, fair-skinned, half Chinese and Jamaican. She was the unit coordinator and immediately we became very close friends.

She truly inspired me and the day I accepted her invite to church, was the day my life changed. Anna was very kind and soft spoken. She was a very humble woman.

We trusted and respected each other. We partied a lot together and shared so many secrets. Attending church together was the only thing we didn't do together. I admired her belief in God, dedication to the Bible and loyalty to Greater Mount Hebron. That was the first church I joined. Every day she sat at the desk and read her Bible. I was so inspired by her. After six months of friendship, she popped the question.

"When are you coming to church with me?"
Anna always wanted me to come to church with her.
"Well right now I work every Sunday because I have school during the week and dance five nights a week. Girl sometimes I come here directly from dancing."
"Well that is not the only day you can attend. Anyway I am not going to stop asking."
"That's fine."

Eventually Anna popped the question again and I surrendered. For whatever reason, I was afraid to attend church. I attended church a great deal when I was a kid, but after Mama and Daddy separated, I stopped. I visited a church by my place a couple of times, but never went back.

Spring 1998
"Hey Anna."
"Hey girl. Are you ready for church yet?
"Yeah I'm ready. I'm off every other weekend so I can go now."
"Good. So will you be there this Sunday."
"Yeah that's cool. Well I gotta go draw a patient."
"Okay."
As I walked down the corridor of Six North East, I saw Craig. Craig worked in administration and he was responsible for making my schedule.

"Craig can I come down to your office and talk to you after I finish with this patient?"
"Sure Kelley. Just come on down when you're done."
"Okay."
Knock, knock.
"Come in."
"What can I do for you Kelley?"
"Well I was wondering if there were any full time positions available?"
"Not right now, but I have one coming up in November."
"Can I have it?"
"Sure. I'll just have to do some paperwork, but it won't be a problem."
"Okay. Thank you very much."

Summer 1998
I no longer worked every Sunday and was ready to attend church. Greater Mount Hebron was located on eightieth and Wood Street. This was the church I began to praise and understand God. Pastor Ledbetter always gave a great sermon and many that I needed.
"Hey girl. I made it. I told you I was going to come today."
"Hey girl. I'm so glad to see you."
Anna gave me a big hug and then posted herself on stage to sing with the choir. I cried throughout the entire sermon. All those negative feelings haunted me and I wanted them gone. I stood up and clapped to the beat of the music.
GOD please come into my life and help me; help me become a better person. Help me see me for the person that I am not the person Mama, Daddy, Nippy, Chrissy and Daminea made me feel to be. I need you God. I'm tired of being miserable and depressed. I need your help. Help me God please. Please God. I need a new way of life. I need something good. Please come into my body and show me who you are. Help me with my thoughts. Teach me how to love myself and forgive.

I prayed. I smiled. I cried. I joined Greater Mount Hebron that very same day and Sunday after Sunday I attended until I received what I searched for. My life changed after that day.****

"Chrissy do you mind if I live with you for about eight months? I'm going back to work full-time in November and I'm going to quit dancing. I will be gone by February of next year."
"That's fine."

I wish Mama's apartment was big enough. I thought. I wanted to start over and move to a different neighborhood. The gangs, violence and drug dealers in my neighborhood were more than I could handle. I lived there for seven years and although I had some very good times there, there were also so many bad memories. I wanted to start fresh somewhere else. I didn't want to move with Chrissy since I hated the sight of her, but I did what I had to do to get out of that neighborhood.
Over the last few years Chrissy and I really didn't have a relationship, but I dealt with her because we were family. I still didn't trust her and definitely didn't want to live in the same house as her. A couple of days before I moved in with her I cried and cried. I left all my belongings in my car. I felt like Chrissy was the same person that treated me like garbage. Eventually I moved in and stayed out of her way. That wasn't hard since I did work, dance, and attend school and church. Four months passed and on October eighteenth, nineteen ninety eight. I had five shows scheduled and gave all of them away. I was tired of men lusting over my body like I was a video vixen. I couldn't tolerate the aggressive behavior. I didn't feel safe anymore and I wanted to be loved for me, not my body. I called my pager and changed my voice mail message.

Hi you have reached Ms. Sexable and as of today I will no longer dance. Please do not page me anymore since I will not be returning any calls. I enjoyed dancing for these last three years, but my time has come to an end. Thank you for all your time.

In November I resumed full time work at U of C hospital. Three months later in February of 1999, I moved to Calumet Park into a one bedroom apartment. This apartment was very nice and clean; no roaches, water bugs or mice. No gang bangers, drug dealers or violence on my block. It was very peaceful and quiet. I was very pleased with my new neighborhood and apartment.

I still struggled with promiscuity, self-esteem and self-love. However, I knew I was finally on the road to happiness. From the time I discovered I was molested, I began to research pedophiles and all areas of abuse. I watched the Oprah Winfrey show whenever the topic was concerning someone being molested or abused. I even called her show and was invited to come on and discuss my issues. However, I would have been an audience participant. I declined the offer. All of this was very therapeutic for me. I didn't stay in therapy for long; maybe a few months. Between church, research and the Oprah Winfrey show, neither Chrissy nor Daminea could make me think I was to blame for being molested. Being molested and abused no longer plagued my mind. I had the knowledge and the truth on my side. The truth was excruciating, but it set me free.

My First Love-11

I was in the last four months of internship for Medical Laboratory Technician. I worked hard over these last two years and finally all my hard work and dedication paid off in May nineteen ninety nine. I was the first person in my family to receive an Associate degree. The sad part about it was Daddy died two months before. I was proud and hurt, but I didn't stop there. I went on to Chicago State University and obtained my Bachelors of Science degree and once again, the first in the family. I never stopped attending church and praising God. My past no longer dominated my present. At this point I knew I wasn't what my family made me to believe I was. In my eyes, they were all miserable and ignorant. I finally accepted my past and owned it. My past was now just my past and it no longer plagued my mind. I never forgot it, but was able to move forward and live life the best way I knew how. However, I still struggled with insecurities until I met my first love.

Summer 1999
"Excuse me, can you tell me why you squat down so far?"
That was the first question I asked Daniel not knowing after that day we would spend seven years together and produce a beautiful young boy. Bally's Total Fitness in Calumet City was where I met Daniel Davis and he was one fine man. I watched him squat on the hack squat machine and his behind almost touched the ground.
"I squat all the way down so that I work my entire butt and make it tighter."
"Oh. Do you mind giving me a spot while I try?"
"Sure."
I walked over to the hack squat machine and pretended as if I didn't know what I was doing. I wanted to be close to Daniel. We talked about exercising and agreed to have lunch. We took a stroll through Frank's department store and I was so nervous.
"What does a fine woman like you want with me?"
"Well you're fine too."

I turned around and looked at him. Daniel and I exchanged numbers and became friends. We met at Bally's daily and worked out together. We became gym junkies and worked so hard together we could have done a commercial. We partied hard and danced together. We lived life as if no one else existed. Daniel was in a relationship and I had recently left someone. Daniel confided in me almost every day we saw each other. He told me some of his most private moments and even cried to me. He was in a very dark place when I met him. The fact that he trusted and confided in me made me feel important. No man other than Josh thought enough of me to express himself to me in such a way. I held his hand and told him everything would be okay. As time passed, Daniel and I became very close and I had the opportunity to enlighten him about my past.

August 1999
Daniel attended church with me and finally I found what I had been searching for.

God please come into my body, please, I need you God. Please show me how powerful you are. I prayed. The Lord entered my body and took over. The Holy Spirit had surfaced. That feeling was greater than what any flesh could ever make me feel. Lord Almighty God, the spirit is and was more powerful than anything or anyone. I desired and needed that to begin my spiritual exploration. I was one hundred percent sure life was guaranteed to be better for me.

"You're a good woman and I don't deserve someone like you. You're smart and beautiful. You have my best interest at heart. I've never had a woman like you. I love you and if I didn't have so much baggage I would marry you in a heartbeat. I have never lived and had so much fun with any other woman. Where I'm weak you're strong. We complement each other. You're very thorough, firm and determined. When you commit to something or someone you give one hundred percent. You don't sit around and wait for things to happen, you make things happen. You have qualities any man would appreciate and if they don't something is wrong with them, not you."

After two years of dating, I was so in love with Daniel. I wanted a child by him and only him. I wanted to take a part of him with me in case we separated. Daniel taught me more than I could ever thank him for. He was the second most instrumental man in my life. He made me see that I was a good and beautiful person. He made me realize that I was stronger than before. He made me realize that I could love and trust men. He was the first man I was able to connect with on an intimate level and not think about being molested.

I hold Daniel close to my heart; not because I have a child by him, but because of what he gave me. Still to this day, like Josh, he has never judged me based on my past or used it maliciously against me. Daniel still tells me he's very grateful to have me in his life and that he loves me. Daniel understands that I was misguided. He understands that I am a strong, remarkable and beautiful woman who rose above and beyond my deadly past. As long as I have breath in my body, I will always be there for Daniel and support him in any way I can. I firmly believe God places people in your life for a reason and Daniel's purpose was to show me that I was capable of loving and trusting again. His purpose was to show me all men are not Nippy.

Today my relationship with Daniel is unconditional. We share stories and respect each other. He has moved on and so have I, but I still trust him with my life. Although we split up, I still love him dearly. Sure he has made numerous mistakes, but all has been forgiven. I might say mean things about him when I'm upset, but aren't we all guilty of that? I do not hold on to any negative energy today. I have learned to let go and truly let God.

Reflecting Back and Moving Forward-12

What type of father disposes uncooked, non-spoiled food like its garbage? Daddy was completely damaged. He wasn't financially broke, but he was definitely broken. Daddy was very abusive and honestly not a good father. He had a gambling habit that took precedence over our needs. I'm not justifying his actions, but his problem was far more complex than I could imagine. I will not judge him, but I will say he was a prime example of someone allowing their past experiences to dominate their life in a negative way.

Daddy exhibited major signs of being broken, damaged and a product of his own demons. The use of a gun on his son wasn't necessary. I do not understand the anger that filled Daddy's heart when David hit him, but I don't think the use of a gun was necessary. I really don't believe Daddy wanted to kill David. Do you actually think Daddy would've been able to live with that guilt? Surely he did some terrible things, but he wasn't made of stone. Daddy used violence to control situations. That was his way of solving problems, while creating more. I loved my father, but I didn't agree with his violent and abusive ways. I surely didn't agree with him beating Mama. Fortunate for me, I never witnessed it.

Now let's think for a moment, Daddy didn't come out of the womb saying he would beat his spouse and abuse his children. Something happened along the way. Was it his upbringing, World War II, or just his lack of dealing with stress? I can't answer that since Daddy never fully explained to me what Grandma did to him and how bad his experience in World War II was. I can only say that he made some terrible mistakes as we all have. I loved him with all my heart and miss him dearly.

Was David wrong for hitting Daddy? Yes. According to God, when a child disobeys and disrespects their parents he will live an unfulfilling life. However, after years of abuse one is bound to snap. Let's use a battered woman for example. After years of being abused, eventually she will cause some serious damage to her husband or kill him. So now we have the Battered Women Syndrome used for defense in Domestic Violence cases. I've heard several people threaten to put their child six feet deep if he or she ever hits them. I'm guilty of that. I can't speak for anyone else, but I doubt very seriously that I would kill my son if he ever hits me. But, he will understand not to ever do that again. At any rate, Daddy may have not physically killed David, but he destroyed his soul and that lead to years of pain and suffering and ultimately his death.

Although Daddy sent me to live with Chrissy, at least he stayed in my presence somewhat. He didn't disappear like Mama. I loved and forgave Daddy. I know he was wrong for blaming me as a child as well as I know he could have continued to take care of me. Unfortunately, he lacked the confidence needed and for that, I was sent to live with Chrissy. The thing that makes me understand his abnormal mentality was the fact that I know Daddy was a child molester. He was just as sick as Nippy. I also know he was abused by his mother, to what extent, I'm not sure. If Daddy could molest his daughter and shoot at his son, I don't think me living with a pedophile would bother him.

Daddy may not have understood forgiveness, but I did and with that I was able to completely forgive him and move forward. We lived a good life as father and daughter until the day he died. Daddy needed me later in life and I'm glad I was able to move forward and be there for him. Everyone deserves a second chance and no one deserves to suffer. God bless his soul.

The fact that Mama wasn't there for me, made me believe she didn't love me. I blamed her because she "Abandoned" me and lacked the strength to tell Bert to go to hell when he said I couldn't live with them. Moreover, she should have never put a man before me. Mama was given a second chance to save me when she arrived at Hyde Park when I was sick. Instead of taking me back to Nippy's house, she had a responsibility to take me with her; instead, she caved in to another man's power, her selfish needs and failed me. Mama was in the same boat I was in. She was also looking for love. She was just as uneducated as I was. Mama wanted to be loved and it is no wonder she couldn't enlighten me about sex, love and relationships. However, she did the best she could. Neither Grandma, nor Granddaddy taught her about love in a relationship. They abused her as well as Daddy did. She was lost just like me; yearning and "Desperately Seeking Love" searching for acceptance and trying to fill a large hole that was deep within the pit of her soul.

I learned so much about what happened to Mama when she was younger and my heart was broken. Mama was raped by her stepfather as well as two young boys. Her first daughter was taken away from her by grandma and placed for adoption. Mama was depressed and looking for a way out when she met Daddy. Not knowing that the abuse would continue, but far worse. She was very dependent upon Daddy. She never finished high school and has never worked. She really didn't think there was a way out until she met Bert. He was her escape.

When Mama left and allowed Bert to deny me, she was simply trying to save her own life. She wanted love and freedom and with that I understood. I know Mama loved me and if she had been able to care for me on her own, she would have left Daddy and took me with her. She was still relying on someone to care for her and with that came him making all the decisions and controlling Mama. Although she found more abuse with Bert, she was strong enough to leave sooner than later.

Mama apologized to me and admitted where she was wrong and I forgave her. I realized how much pain Mama suffered from her past abuse and I didn't want to be an addition to that. I know some of you would say that I shouldn't have cared about her abuse or illness based on how she abandoned and chose a man over me. Well it's not my place to be her judge and jury. Surely I suffered for the sins of Mama and Daddy, but I made it. When you really forgive someone you learn to let go, love and build a new relationship based on today not yesterday.

Mama's diagnosis with Hepatitis was crucial and she needed me more than ever in the upcoming years and I was more than eager to give her the love, commitment and the loyalty she desired. I cherished and honored Mama. I do not regret showing her not one ounce of love. There was no way I was about to leave my mother high and dry. I needed to forgive her. I would have missed out on all the beautiful years we shared. I would have missed out on the times of my life with Mama if I held on to that negative energy. We went on double dates, partied and shopped together. Mama and I also enjoyed dinner dates and late night snacks. Since I didn't, I had the opportunity to know and love Mama for who she was regardless of all the mistakes she made. We had our moments, but the past never affected our relationship again. God bless her soul. (R.I.P)

Daminea introduced me to cigarettes, alcohol, marijuana, sex, lesbianism and incest. Making me perform oral sex on her was the most disgusting. This is very disturbing. The first thought that comes to my mind is where Daminea; a thirteen year old learn this behavior? I know the answer to that, but before I tell you, my next question is, was Daminea conscious of what she was doing? Sure. She was aware of spreading her legs and she knew it would satisfy her and she knew it was wrong. My next question is did she know it was referred to as Incest? No. Did she care? No. The only thing that mattered to Daminea at that time was sexual gratification.

Back to my first question, where did Daminea learn this behavior? Daddy of course, however, I will not indulge into Daminea's world as a victim. Just understand she was introduced into a life of incest, lies, abuse, manipulation and betrayal before I was born.

Daminea caused me plenty of mental anguish and my mind was distorted. I was too young to enjoy any sexual acts and so was she. I'm not justifying her behavior, but she was not taught to be a role model. These experiences laid the foundation for my curiosity about men and women at a later date in my life. The fact that I was coerced into being with girls so much, I began to like and enjoy it. I thought about being with women sexually and was totally confused throughout life until I acted on those feelings at twenty eight years old. At that point I indulged on a regular basis.

As far as marijuana, I truly enjoyed the feeling it gave me. Neither Mama, nor Daddy ever told me not to use drugs or drink alcohol. Being introduced at nine years-old lead to another thirteen years of smoking it, however, I finally quit at twenty two years old. Although I enjoyed using marijuana, that's not to say I condone the use of any drug because I don't. Today I get high off of life and the blessings God has granted me. Cigarettes; Lord knows that this is one habit I wish I was never introduced to. It is truly an addiction. If you have never smoked cigarettes please don't ever try and until you have walked in a smoker's shoe don't judge them.

I look back and I question, how did I wind up being left alone with "Chester the Molester?" Some questions will never be answered. Tyrone Brown Sr. was a known pedophile and from what I know about predators today, he manipulated Daminea to get to me and regain my friendship. Of course Mama and Daddy were gone because I know Mama wouldn't have let me go anywhere with him. Nippy was one clever pedophile as they all are. The mere fact that Daminea was too young for him was his advantage. He knew he could influence her to do whatever he wanted. So the truth be told, Damenia, Nicki and I were all molested by Tyrone Brown Sr. Tyrone Brown Sr. was never Damenia's boyfriend.

I know today Daminea would have never taught me these things if she had been taught better. The things she learned and experienced were inappropriate for any child. She was only doing what she was taught and for that I understand how she could have experimented with me and the other children in our neighborhood. Do I have any regrets? Not at all. Have I forgiven Daminea? Entirely. I love her and I pray for her peace today.

Like Mama, Chrissy was in a very abusive relationship; one that almost led to her death. She too was looking for love and since it wasn't taught in our home, she accepted years of abuse and inflicted years on me. Not only that, as I explained in my story, abuse was taught more than anything in my home.

This was a vicious cycle that started before I was born. Everyone before me had already been conditioned to either accepting more abuse or abusing others. Chrissy was in pain from what Daddy did to her and was filled with anger. I just happened to be her victim.

Living with Chrissy was really no different from living with my parents. The only exception was that Chrissy was on drugs and with that decisions are never wisely made. I'm not making excuses for her behavior. I am simply explaining what led me to forgive her.

I never figured out why Chrissy evicted me and not Nicki. I never understood why she protected Nicki and not me. Maybe she really thought I knew what I was doing. Maybe she didn't understand what child molestation is. I'm sure she didn't just like Damenia didn't understand incest. However, if she put me out for allegedly having "sex" with Nippy, why didn't she put Nicki out? She helped and protected her from Nippy. I wanted to be helped, but instead I was thrown to the wolves. That alone made me lose all respect for her and it really took quite some time for her to regain my trust and respect.

Chrissy was twenty-two years old and very aware of the decision she made to evict me. Did she care? No more than Daddy cared when he evicted her. I watched Daddy abuse Chrissy numerous times and she repeated that vicious cycle on me. Does it make it right that her abusive behavior was a learned condition? Not at all. Chrissy knew enough to protect and support Nicki, so therefore, she should've protected me. Several times I asked Chrissy for an apology and she refused. She continued to blame me. It doesn't bother me what she thinks today since I know the "Truth". There was nothing on this earth I could have done to deserve that type of treatment. No more than she deserved what Daddy did to her. Only Chrissy knows why she treated me so poorly. I hated her for a long time and today I don't need an apology or reasons to justify her behavior. I know it was wrong. I also know we do what we are taught. As the years passed and I began to understand more about Chrissy and how she was mirror image to Mama, I learned to forgive her. Our relationship isn't perfect, but I understand why she did the things she did to me. I love her and wish her nothing, but peace, love and happiness in her life.

As far as Tyrone Brown Sr. aka Nippy "Chester the Molester" is concerned, I can only pray for him since he was truly one mentally sick individual. He raped my mind, body and soul. He intentionally manipulated me and made me believe my family didn't love me. He stole my virginity and my teenage years. For many years, I hated him. I despised him for what he had done to me and my family. Lord knows if I had seen him crossing any street, I would've made him a hood ornament and pleaded insanity in court. It sounds premeditated and it would have been. He definitely planned his attack on me and was malicious enough to say it boldly. He knew he was a pedophile. He preyed on young girls and I definitely wanted to extinguish him.

Being forced to live with a predator and not having anyone to save me was very depressing and wrong. Eventually, I thought I loved him. I thought he was my friend. I thought he loved me. I thought these were the right things to do. Believe it or not, in most cases victims develop these "unnatural" emotions for his or her abuser. It's really a trick of the mind from being manipulated. The most important thing to remember and understand is your mind didn't like the actions, your body did. This is exactly how an abuser shifts the blame onto the victim. Don't be fooled any longer, it was NEVER your fault.

Tyrone Brown Sr. definitely committed a crime against me; Statutory Rape, however, we all deserve a second chance at life. I just hope he has allowed God to make changes in his. Have I forgiven Nippy? Indeed I have. He controlled me for numerous years and I refuse to remain his victim. I forgave him for myself. I forgave him because I needed to rid myself of the negative emotions that controlled my life. I forgave him because it was the right thing to do. If not, I may very well have continued to be sexually abused by him. Who knows what happened in his life to make him mentally unstable and honestly, I really don't care. The only thing that matters to me is that I am free. Nippy no longer has power over me. Praise God.

Reflecting back on my relationship with Josh I must have been truly messed up. How pathetic is it to date a married man or woman for that matter? I didn't know any better. I was wrecking a God created union and had no remorse. How could I have remorse when I was never conscious of the immoral mistake I was making? My self-esteem was invisible. I thought I was in love with a married man and never loved myself. If I truly loved and respected myself, I would have never subjected myself to such pain and agony. However, pain and agony was a place very well known to me. I was dead wrong for disrupting his family and causing his wife any pain. I was young, uneducated, selfish, misplaced and searching for love and it didn't matter where I received it. I needed it. I had no right dating Josh and my deepest apology to Beth.

Understand that I am fully aware of the fact that Josh was also responsible. Nevertheless, that was a learning experience for me. As long as I have breath in my body nothing will make me stoop to such a level again. I respect the sacred foundation of marriage as well as I respect myself. I'm no longer misplaced and hopeless for someone to love me because I love myself. I only pray that when God blesses me with a husband, karma doesn't come around and slap me in the face.

Today Josh and I are good friends and all has been forgiven. I have a vast amount of respect for him and that respect is reciprocated. Josh has never used my past to hurt me. He understands living in darkness. Josh understands that my past is where it is and does not represent my present. He understands that I was misguided and a product of severe abuse. Today Josh speaks highly of me and recognizes that I am a survivor. He refers to me as remarkable.

My experience with stripping was an exciting, but dangerous one. I stripped and exposed my body to men everywhere and for that I lacked total respect for myself. My body is a temple and not to be exposed for monetary gain. Am I ashamed of it? Not at all. I enjoyed entertaining and making those men smile, not to mention, the money was great and it helped me get through school. Dancing gave me a sense of self-love. The very fact that I didn't indulge in any sexual activities while performing made me feel good about me. The fact that hundreds of men and women requested my show made me feel loved. As bizarre as this may be, the attention I received from my clients was a boost for my self-esteem. Any form of love and appreciation was needed at that time in my life.

On the contrary, the world of stripping could have been hazardous to my health. The drugs, prostitution, lesbianism and the money could have all gained control of me. But, that was not what I searched for or needed. The abuse I experienced eventually led to me abusing myself. I was only familiar with abuse and so assuming sex was a direct connection to love was the only way I knew how to express myself. However, today I am very knowledgeable about sex and love. Although they do go hand-in-hand, sex should never be indulged in if you're looking for love in return. It's such a powerful experience and causes many emotions to manifest and surface; emotions that young women or men are not mentally capable of dealing with maturely. I didn't know what making love entailed. I only knew what I was taught. What I was taught was wrong and could have definitely led me to a life of complete misery, confusion and ultimately my demise. The idea of sleeping who over one hundred men tells me I was "Desperately Seeking Love." There is no way a woman will allow herself to be used up and asserts she loves herself. That's like combining oil and water, it doesn't mix. It's impossible to love and respect yourself and sleep with over one hundred men. But, let's remove that number for one second. If a woman really loves and respects herself, casual sex with anyone other than a significant partner or spouse will be null and void.

That sounds like someone who has been misguided, naïve or searching for love and of course, in all the wrong places. The fact that I caused pain to some of my partners tells me I was in pain myself. Why else would someone cause intentional pain to anyone? Not to mention, thinking I was in charge was complete confusion. I caused pain to men who didn't hurt me and I still felt empty. I lost complete control and hated myself. The abuse I endured left a very negative impact on my psyche. My mind was raped over and over again. It left me wide open for additional abuse. I was confused for many years and I never knew why I treated myself so poorly. I suffered from low self-esteem, guilt, promiscuity, lack of respect, suicidal ideations and attempts, identity crisis, alcohol and marijuana abuse and more than I care to remember. This promiscuous lifestyle could have ruined my life in numerous ways such as HIV or some other incurable disease, prostitution or maybe even death.

I know most of you would just label me as a slut and that's acceptable to me. Fortunately for me, your thoughts are irrelevant. I suggest you do your research on victims of Incest, Sexual, Mental, Physical and Verbal abuse. I started to believe all the negative connotations that Chrissy, Daminea and Nippy said to me. They tarnished my mind. I felt like garbage after discovering my virginity was stolen by a pedophile. I felt even worse after being blamed. These experiences took a very pessimistic toll on my life and mind. As stated before, I wanted my demise to approach me immediately. Apparently I'm not good at suicide. It would have been an easy way out as well as selfish. However, I thought it was the best solution for my severe mental distress. I was wrong. Suicide is never the answer; it is a permanent solution for a temporary problem.

Today promiscuity doesn't exist in my life. I love who I am and I now know that sex is not a direct connection to love. My self-esteem is great and I don't need a man's love to feel complete. I am whole. It is God's love that I need, not flesh. Sure we all need companionship, but we must love ourselves in order to really appreciate and accept someone else's love. Though I speak of women, this also applies to men.

Back then I wish my parents would have protected and loved me. I wish Nippy would have never been allowed in our home. I wish Mama would have never abandoned me. I wish Damenia would have never made me perform oral sex on her or force me to engage in sexual acts with boys and girls. I wish Chrissy would have never thrown me out. I wish I had someone to guide me in a more positive direction. Someone that would've told me that sex was not the way to find love and sex without mutual emotions was just sex. I wish someone would have taught me to respect and love myself. But **what happened, has happened** and the past cannot be changed.

Maybe this was the road that GOD has blessed me with so that he could use me to open hearts, cleanse mind and break the chain of abuse. Maybe GOD allowed the Devil to intervene and set forth his plan. Maybe the Devil Perfectly Planned my life and it was meant for my demise. Maybe GOD was testing my faith. Maybe it was all a test. Maybe GOD tested me from the very beginning to determine if I would make the right decisions later on in life, even though, I was misled from the beginning. Because of the sins of my parents, I suffered and GOD provided me with enough strength to continue to move forward throughout each stage of my life and each stage of abuse. So today, HE is the reason I am who I am. HE is the reason I have overcome what most individuals won't even speak of. He is the reason the one thing that could have destroyed me is the one thing I am most passionate about.

I have cultivated the minds of many who had no hope or were confused, scared and unwilling to trust. My life is a springboard for others to know that not only can one survive abuse, but one can also become victorious. Today, I have a broad array of knowledge and experience on abuse and that makes me capable of writing this book. I can now inspire, guide or motivate some other Kelley Porters out here waiting for help. Some other misguided or abandoned individuals or victims of sexual abuse or domestic violence that just needs to hear,

You can do it. You're going to be okay. I can help. You are beautiful and smart. You are not worthless. You are important. Just hang in there. I am here if you ever need to talk. I'm proud of you or simply, I love you.

The tongue is a very powerful weapon and if used inappropriately, many souls and minds can be severely altered. If used appropriately, lives can be uplifted and encouraged and ultimately the chain of abuse can be broken. All the money, traveling and materialistic growth was nothing compared to the love I felt from GOD. None of that touched my soul. The love I felt from the grace of God helped me to forgive and move forward. I trusted and believed in GOD and with that, I learned to believe in me and know that I am loved. I am beautiful. I am a Victor. I was not, nor have I ever been what my abusers accused me to be. I made it and they can never hurt me again..

The purpose of this chapter is to encourage victims who have not forgiven their abusers to "Reflect Back;" to learn and understand and "Move Forward;" to live.

"Reflect Back" to understand what happened and learn from it. Trauma such as abuse cannot be avoided. It must be dealt with. One cannot suppress this pain forever and believe he or she will live a WHOLE, fulfilling life. It is impossible. Surely one can be successful, wealthy and married with children. That sounds like a fulfilling life, but, I can guarantee deep within the individual who was abused, their soul is broken and every day they are reminded of the deep rooted issues that are buried. Every day your spouse is questioning your behaviors, but can't pinpoint the problem.

Eventually, these issues have to be dealt with and at that point your life will either crumble or elevate. The choice is yours and I hope you choose wisely. If not, expect the rest of your life to be lived in pieces. By definition I mean, with pain, there is still anger. With silence, there is a crying voice. With a void, there is no compassion. With fear, there is no liberation. Without forgiveness, there is no completion of love. Without honesty, there is deceit. Without understanding, there is no peace. Without faith, there is no healing.

Move Forward to Live. After you have "Reflected Back" it is now time to "Move Forward" to Live. By definition I mean, nothing in the past can affect your present or future. Everything that has occurred in your past life is now an experience that you can share with someone else to inspire them. You will live in the present day and no longer will you reflect on past pain when faced with struggles. No longer will you allow your past to prevent you from loving or trusting. You will believe in you. You will have faith and believe that you are important and worthy of happiness. You will now look forward to the many blessings that are ahead and take pride in being you.

Forgiveness – 13

Spring 2008
I have bared my heart and soul to you and can only hope that if anyone has ever experienced severe abuse as I have or are currently experiencing any form of abuse, you will reach out for help. I encourage you to be strong and I encourage you to start the healing process that begins with forgiveness.

Please do understand that abuse left unforgiven is dangerous to the soul. Maybe we all can't afford therapy, but do reach out for help. It is difficult to move forward if you harvest and dwell in what God only wanted us to learn from. Reach out to someone, a friend, relative, teacher, pastor, doctor or nurse or just simply pray every day and believe that God or someone will listen and be more than willing to help. I know some of us don't believe in the power of prayer, but trust me it really works. I didn't forgive my abusers because I wanted to. I forgave them because it was the correct course of action and because God commanded me. I asked God to forgive them and myself for all the sins I committed during this tragic time in my life. It was a difficult task and it took years, but I accomplished it. Subsequently, it was like a ton of boulders lifted from my shoulders. All feelings of anger, bitterness and resentment turned into relief. I am free. Now, I would like to enlighten you on forgiveness because at heart, the goal of my book is to inspire you to forgive the people who have caused you great pain. To inspire you to take control and not allow your past negative experiences to dominate your life. To inspire you to live with a cleansed heart and a free mind. To inspire you to forgive, not forget, just simply LET GO.

For me forgiveness was letting go of all the pain that was placed upon me by my abusers. Forgiveness for me was to become free of hate, pain and resentment. Forgiveness was the start of a new beginning. What would I have gained if I had sought vengeance, committed suicide, homicide or remained depressed and angry? What would life have been like for me?

I can assure you I would not be happy or writing this book. Forgiveness was finding peace with all the negative energy that consumed me. Forgiveness was accepting, owning and appreciating my past life. My past is a part of me and always will be. My past is not just my past; it has brought me to self-love. I am a good woman. I am strong and I am liberated. Finally I love who I am, past, present, flaws and all.

Forgiveness is a need for the soul to survive. Without it we live in darkness where, anger, pain and rage accumulate and will annihilate our souls. We have to learn to forgive and let go of the wrong that was done to us. It takes a strong spiritual connection to really forgive and become free. If you cannot accomplish this it will be difficult to move forward. You may as well be locked into the situation that caused you to live in this dark hole. Without forgiveness your mental state is jeopardized. Your mind is not free to cultivate. How can you live up to your fullest potential if you live in darkness that was placed upon us to learn from and not dwell? We live in a world where the negative experiences are just as abundant as the positive, if not more. All of them are blessings. Someone is guaranteed to wrong you again. Free you, forgive yourself and forgive others. Forgiveness is a powerful tool because it liberates the soul.

This is my truth and all has been forgiven. This book is not meant to inflict pain upon any member of my family. No grief, no anger, no lies, no hate, only love. It would be unfortunate for any of my relatives or anyone to be offended. Any anger expressed from my story only informs me that one has not forgiven themselves. One has not accepted his or her past as a blessing and a tool to bring us closer to self-love. We are God's children and are not to blame. We were victims of severe abuse that began before Mama and Daddy. Trust me if they knew better, they would have done better. My truth is only meant to aid in the process of forgiveness and evolution. I evolved from an abused child, teenager and young adult into a strong, loving parent, sister, aunt, daughter, individual and friend with compassion for others. I broke the chain.

My son has never experienced any abuse delivered from my hands and I will die before I allow someone to inflict pain upon him.

Too many men and women have experienced a life of abuse as I have and many of them are uncertain of how to advance. Most people would wonder how I made it. I made it because God has walked along side of me from the beginning. I am a Victor. I am my mother and father's child. I believed and held on to those deeply and softly spoken words, *I love you*. Without God and the family he positioned me in, I would not be who I am today. God placed me in my family to be a leader and set examples when others could not. I came from nothing, mentally, financially, and spiritually. But, I rose above and beyond most individual's understanding. I am rich; not with money, but in my heart and mind. My heart is clean and free of the negative feelings and thoughts. I own everything that I experienced, however, it did not break me, it made me. All of my trials and tribulations have made me who I am, a proud black woman giving back and hoping one day someone will read this book and start the process of forgiving his or her abuser(s) and become what God wanted us to be; in the eyes of him.

If I had to go back and change anything in my life, what would I change? Nothing at all. My life was a blessing and now it's time for me to pay it forward. I have no regrets. All of my positive and negative blessings were for me to learn from. If you have suffered any of the abuse I have written about, I urge you to use God's tools. Prayer and therapy really do work.

I live freely and have no concern for what others think of me. Their thoughts have no bearing on my life. To judge me or maliciously attempt to use my past against me only informs me that one is ignorant and deserves to be dismissed from my life.

To throw my past in my face only informs me that you do not understand the after effects of abuse. If you truly understood what abuse does to the mind, you would have compassion and understanding. I have been successful in convincing several individuals in praying and obtaining therapy. I strongly believe if I successfully convinced them to see that their past was dominating their present, then this book can definitely do the same. I will continue to speak out about abuse and attempt to inspire and empower as many as I can.

To forgive is to set a prisoner free and discover the prisoner was YOU. Matthew 6:14, 15.

I believe in order for any individual to obtain the strength needed to forgive any source of struggle, he or she will have to do the following.

Grieve - Be Sad/Cry
- In most cases victims of abuse attempt to suppress the pain. Instead of dealing with or grieving they tend to place it deep in their souls and hope it will go away. The problem with that is as long as the pain is manifested, it will surface. Now this leads to more problems because new relationships will be affected. Individuals who have nothing to do with this struggle or pain will feel the wrath from it.
- Without grieving the heart is bitter and the soul is compromised. By definition I mean the same pain you felt while being abused or hurt is the same pain that will almost immediately surface. Why? Because every new individual is being compared to the wrongdoer instead of looking at the situation for TODAY. A tarnished heart will always retreat to past pain.
- Grieving does not mean going into a depression. It means to have your days of sadness. "RELEASE IT" Don't hold onto the pain. *Every tear shed is a sign of*

Strength and Freedom to come. Have your five minutes of self-pity and keep going.

Understanding/Compassion - Understand that WE all are sinners.
I know it's difficult to have compassion or understanding for any child molester or for anyone that hurts you so this is the part of forgiveness that makes it so hard to accomplish. How many times have you hurt someone? We are all human and we all make mistakes. Whether it was with intent or inadvertently, we all err. How did you feel after you hurt someone and he or she held a grudge against you? Deep in your heart you wanted that person to feel your pain and understand that you needed deliverance as well. A scorned heart will always cause pain. One has to understand that this individual needs to heal as well. This is a broken soul. After the tears have faded, the wrongdoer can longer control your everyday emotions. Therefore, it is now time to look into your heart and realize that you are not perfect either. Understand that WE are all sinners and the same compassion you want someone to have for you, is the same compassion and understanding you must be willing to offer.

Acceptance - What happened; has happened and will not change. Accept the fact that you were deeply hurt and may be left with scars. Accept the fact that it will be difficult to move forward, but you can. Accept the fact that life is filled with wrongdoers and as long as you live someone will hurt you again. After you offer some compassion and understand that it is okay, you only have two choices; live bitter or happy. The choice is yours.

Accountability - Be responsible for your own actions.
When an adult survivor of child abuse accepts their responsibility, forgiveness becomes easy. That "Little Girl or Boy" was accountable; accountable for not being able to save him or herself. Survivors must utilize these same steps in order to forgive that little person who was incapable of saving

you from the predator.

When an adult stays in a situation that they know is completely toxic, it is their responsibility to realize that he or she was just as at fault as the wrongdoer was. Your job was to get help or get out. If you chose not to then be accountable and admit what you could have done different. Don't place blame on others when you know you could've done better. Placing blame denies you the opportunity to learn from this horrific experience therefore leading to repeated history.

Learn From It - Find Something Positive
One of the key elements of forgiveness is to learn from the pain. There is a lesson in everything we experience. It doesn't matter how bad, malicious or callous, there is a lesson. To learn from hurt is to gain strength. To learn from hurt is to gain knowledge. To learn from hurt is growing and maturing. Find something positive and there is always one, only you know. Did you learn something about yourself during this experience? Did it make you a better person? Learn from all experiences, good or bad, they are all blessings.

Survivor -14

When I reflect on the life I endured over the last couple of decades, I realize I am much more than Kelley R. Porter. The tags of mother, lover and friend fit me well, but the most applicable and poignant one is that of a survivor. We probably all have our memories of the unpleasant things that we thought would bring about our demise and personally I wish there was simply one or two. That is not the case. My story is one of two decades of the worst and most despicable acts a human being can endure.

The story I have shared with you has taken me through life's extremes, but nevertheless I emerged confident, forgiving and hopeful. By all accounts many years ago the incest, rape, substance abuse, sexual manipulations and schemes should have brought about my demise. Instead, it helped me surface as a woman who if I did not tell you my story you would never imagine that I spent years dancing in the belly of hell and emerged singed and not burned to a crisp.

One would never know since I have a vibrant personality and am always smiling. This story is nonexistence in my life today and that is why you will find it hard to believe I endured such agony and am the person I am today. I am the real me. The Kelley before the happy go-lucky and innocent child's life was interrupted by complete evil. I remember being a spunky, go-getter when I was a child. I remember being excited to attend school. I remember my family protecting me from evil. But, I also remember what they didn't protect me from. But, that is all right today because I no longer live in turmoil. My smile is real. My confidence is real. My self-security is real. My faith is real and my freedom is real.

When I tell people what I have experienced they are in disbelief. There is always one question in particular. How did you make it out of that? I sometimes cannot believe that the life I lived is actually mine. I look back and ask myself. How did I ever make it out alive? The only answer that comes to me is that God walked along side me the entire way. I never thought in a million years I would be the person I am today. I never thought I would amount to anything much less write this book and share my life. What's more, many times I wanted to end my life and have tried. But, I realize today that life is very precious and although I was thrown many curve balls, I successfully scored a home run.

Today I am blessed to be where I'm at. I'm in a place of peace where my past no longer affects me. I appreciate having experienced all that I have since I love who it has made me become, a survivor. Although I may have triggers, I'm not affected by them anymore. I will never forget what was done to me, but the state of mind I'm in today understands and knows that my life was a blessing so there is no reason to be upset or hurt by what happened years ago. The only way to understand that it was a blessing is to understand God. God never gave me any more than I was capable of handling.

In my story it appeared as if I was headed for my destruction, but apparently that was not in God's plan. The greatest part of being where I am today is that my past no longer controls me and that is what makes me a survivor. There is no need to drink until I forget. There is no need to smoke marijuana and avoid my truth. There is definitely no need to engage in casual sex attempting to find love. There is no void to fill and there absolutely is no more pain. I'm free and it feels so wonderful to be.

My life today is far from perfect, but I know it was Perfectly Planned. I rose above the pain so that I could do exactly what I am doing today. I am a beacon of light to the world.

I experience trials and tribulations today, but I'm confident that if I survived the pits of hell there is nothing I cannot withstand today. I love the place I'm in today. It's a place of peace; a place of new beginnings; a place of freedom; a place of confidence and security and a place of truly loving and knowing who I am. It's a place of maturity and giving back. It's a place of knowing I deserve the best. It's a place of knowing the difference between love and abuse. It's a place of knowing when someone is not good for you. It's a place of knowing how to let go. It's a place of finding positive in all negative. It's a place called survivor.

I am where most victims want to be, but often never understand the path you must take in order to become a survivor. It wasn't easy at all, but it is well worth it in the end. I am proud to say that I survived twenty years of abuse and I am whole. I feel so liberated, it's like the abuse never happened. It's amazing to me that I endured all that pain and is capable of loving today. It's amazing for me to believe that after all that deceit and betrayal, I am capable of trusting again. It's amazing that I did not become an abuser. It's amazing because I am the total opposite of what I could have been and feel free to let your mind wander.

Eleven years ago when I was delivered, I learned to trust and love again. But, I also became closer to self. I refused to give up and allow my life to begin and end in misery. I knew there was more for me to experience like having my first child. I wanted to be liberated and rid of all the nightmares and experience some of the great dreams that I have. One is making a positive change in someone's life. I have that opportunity now because I survived two decades of abuse. There is no way I would be able to share my life with the world if my mind and heart wasn't free of the anger, pain and resentment. I would not be able to receive the blessings I do today if I had not forgiven what was done to me. It feels wonderful to awake and go out into the world a happy woman. It sometimes feels like being reborn.

I started over eleven years ago and I have come a long way. There were some bumps in the roads and more curve balls, but that's another book.

In the present day it is my honor to share my life's experiences with you and I hope if you have been a victim or know someone that has been a victim of abuse today you will take the path of becoming a survivor. Today you will take that journey of freeing yourself and forgiving your abusers. This is what I want for you. I believe it is my duty to use my life and help victims understand that the embarrassment and shame does not belong to you. The depression and non-constructive coping mechanisms are not the answer. The insecurities and self-hate can be turned into confidence and self-love. I believe in you and I want you to believe in you. I believe that you will one day look back and say that was the past but this is my present. I believe that your heart will one day be a forgiving heart. I believe if I did not share with the world what God has brought me through, I would be selfish. There is no way I could survive two decades of unimaginable things and not pay it forward. That is my heart and it is healed and now it's time to heal others with my story.

I am a woman of great passion and love. I sincerely hope my life can touch you in ways that will be forever changing. I hope my story touches every emotion in your body, but the feelings I want to touch within you and get rid of is the anger, pain and bitterness. Those are the emotions that prevent you from becoming a survivor. Those emotions prevent you from loving, giving and from moving forward. Those are the emotions that almost destroyed me. I do not want you to suffer any longer. I want you to become who I am, a survivor and leader pressing and paying it forward. After reading my story, please know that if I made it, then so can you.

I have bared my soul and hope I am able to help someone out of their darkness and into a place of light where forgiveness releases you from the pit of the darkness. I looked back to understand and learn from what happened and now I look ahead to live and give back to those in dire need. Life after abuse is something to celebrate and Perfectly Planned is my celebration to you.

My Personal Thoughts-15

Children are not to be blamed. One reason I wrote this book is for people like you, you know who you are, the ones that blame children, the ones who are just plain ignorant. You are no different than the abuser. Your heads need to be examined. You will probably say, he or she wanted it or why didn't they tell. Well, have you ever heard of manipulating, brainwashing or grooming? How about turning the child against the family? How about threats and, how about giving the child exactly what the parents don't give? Pedophiles seek these inadequacies or neglect in families so they have an easy shot. Those are just a few of the steps a pedophile takes in an effort to attain his goal, penetration. Have you got it yet? I hope so, because if not, God have mercy on your soul.

It's all about education. What you don't know will hurt you. So in essence, please never blame a child for an adult's behavior. Ensure that the adult is held accountable for his or her actions. Support the children and if you cannot; go look in the mirror. You have the problem. What's your problem? Ignorance and it's not bliss, this time. You were either abused and now you are an abuser or someone failed to educate you on what sexual abuse is. So I'm excited you are reading my book. Learn something.

Perfectly Planned Book Discussion

1. Referring to the chapter Chester the Molester, do you think a teenager under the age of seventeen is capable of consensual sex with an adult?

2. How has Perfectly Planned affected you?

3. Referring to the chapter Forgiveness, do you understand how important it is to forgive your abuser?

4. Have you ever been molested and if so, did Perfectly Planned make you understand that guilt and shame does not belong to you?

5. After reading Perfectly Planned, what are the steps one should take if he or she suspects their child has been molested?

6. Referring to the chapter Desperately Seeking Love, has it helped you understand why a victim of abuse will become promiscuous?

7. After reading Perfectly Planned, are you capable of recognizing the signs of a pedophile?

8. After reading Perfectly Planned, are you capable of recognizing the behavioral changes in your child if he or she were molested?

9. Referring to the chapter Abandoned, how did you feel about my mother taking me back to the pedophile's house?

10. After reading Perfectly Planned, how do you make your child feel comfortable enough to tell you that he or she is being fondled by an adult?

11. Referring to the chapter the Ring Leader, do you think Damenia was fully aware of what she was doing or was she doing what she was taught?

12. Referring to the chapter Ms. Sexable the College Student, did you think I would return to school after I quit?

13. After reading the chapter the Ring Leader, do you understand how a child being introduced to the same sex will grow up confused about their sexuality?

14. After reading Perfectly Planned, did it help you understand how childhood sexual abuse can lead to promiscuity, depression and suicide idealizations?

15. Referring to the chapter Shattered Trust, do you understand if a child is blamed initially, why he or she may not tell if approached again by a pedophile?

16. After reading Perfectly Planned, would you allow your thirteen year old to read this book?

17. After reading the chapter on Forgiveness, did it make you revisit or review any issues in your life? If so how?

18. After reading Perfectly Planned, do you understand how childhood abuse affects your adulthood (intimate) relationships if unforgiven?

19. After reading Perfectly Planned, did it make you pay more attention to your children?

20. Referring to the chapter Reflecting Back and Moving Forward, do you understand the importance of revisiting your childhood abuse in order to really move forward?

About The Author

A successful leader and expert on overcoming all forms of abuse, avoiding toxic relationships and the art of forgiveness, Kelley Porter is a Certified Transformation, and Personal Development Coach, Award Winning Six-time Author, and Professional Speaker. As a speaker, Kelley's transparent and authentic style of speaking will empower anyone to self-reflect, start the process of healing and correct thoughts and behaviors that may hinder them from living a healthy and non-toxic lifestyle.

As a Coach, Kelley empowers you to reach emotional freedom, gain clarity and discover your infinite possibilities. She is well known for assisting in the removal of mental and emotional blocks that hinders people from reaching their fullest potential. Her areas of specialty are, but not limited to; abuse, healing, relationships, thoughts, emotions, and behaviors as she has written books on all topics. Kelley has over thirty years of direct experience with all forms of abuse, domestic violence relationships, creating purpose and power from painful experiences, and creating a positive mindset.

Kelley contributes to society her genuine love for healing, improving awareness and identity, developing talents and potential; enhancing the quality of life and the realization of dreams and aspirations. Kelley's mission is to guide you to design a healthy and meaningful life through wisdom, consciousness, self-reflection, self-love, accountability and forgiveness. Prior to Kelley discovering her life purpose, she spent twenty-three years in healthcare and worked fifteen of those years as a Medical Technologist, as she is a member of the American Society for Clinical Pathologist.

Kelley has been seen and heard on radio and TV including WVON, HOT105 (Florida), Inspiration 1390, WKKC, Channel 2, 5, 7 and 19 and My Black is Beautiful (online). She has been featured in Rolling Out Magazine, Chicago Tribune, Bean Soup Times, SisterSpeak237 (Africa) and spoken for numerous prestigious organizations such as Robert H. McKinney Law School and the Chicago Police Department. She is available for speaking engagements such as keynotes, seminars, workshops, conferences and panels. Her audience can range from congregations, universities, youth groups, NFP and community organizations, the educational and prison system as well as shelters.

Kelley Porter

www.ingramcontent.com/pod-product-compliance
Lightning Source LLC
Chambersburg PA
CBHW072004290426
44109CB00018B/2129